Praise for *Before the Nikah*

"Dr. Aneesah Nadir has been an educator and trainer of imams and the Muslim community on family issues. I am so glad she is now putting her knowledge in a book for the average Muslim anywhere to access. I am quite sure people will benefit from her insight and as a result work towards building healthy families and communities."

**Mohamed Hag Magid; Imam,
All Dulles Area Muslim Society
(ADAMS) Center; Coauthor,
Before You Tie the Knot: A Guide for Couples**

"I cannot think of a better person who genuinely supports and reminds us of the path to marital bliss than Dr. Nadir. She is a committed and consistent proponent of love and healthy marriages. As a two time alumna and instructor of the **Before the Nikah** course, Dr. Nadir's dedication to educate students is rooted in her knowledge about the interconnectedness between healthy marriages and healthy families. The book and the course are parallel to each other. What a treat for the reader!!! Dr. Nadir is a regal leader whose body of work continues to shine through just as bright as her commitment to marital tranquility in this life and in the hereafter."

**Latisha K. Ojuriye M.A. , P.D., NCSP ,
CEO Kareem Education Consulting Services, LLC;
Nationally Certified School Psychologist**

"Couples who have been married a long time learn the hard way, so read the book and save yourself a lot of pain and trouble. If you are serious about getting married, then take the first step and buy this book."

**Baba Ali
Co-founder, Half Our Deen**

"Arguably, no author is better suited and positioned than Dr. Aneesah Nadir to write on the topic of marriage preparation within the Islamic tradition. The pioneering work of Nadir in the Muslim American community for more than two decades in the areas of premarital preparation, and pre and post-marital counseling is unparalleled.

Nadir has forced an important conversation on a fundamental principle of the Islamic faith that is considered to be "half of the religion." Before the Nikah is required reading for anyone who wants a step by step guide to this important institution. Things will never be the same again in the conversation and scholarship around marriage in Islam."

Qasim Amin Nathari, Imam
and author of The State of Islam in Black America

As a helping professional who is not Muslim, Dr. Nadir has graciously shared her knowledge about Muslim religion and culture with me so that I can best serve my clients who practice that faith. I would highly recommend her book to any helping professional who is not Muslim and would like to learn more about how to support Muslim singles and couples with healthy relationships.

Joy Carter, LMSW,
Clinical Social Work, Therapist

Congratulations to my colleague for providing us a much needed resource to guide us to this critical act of marriage! Her commitment to increasing the "successful, blessed, and lasting marriage rate among the FAITH COMMUNITY is commendable."

Professor Clay Dix,
Arizona State University West (Retired)

"Divorce rates in our country are astronomical. Unfortunately, the frequency of divorce in the Muslim community is no exception as we witness increasingly large numbers of people we know and love forced to deal with the social, economic and psychological devastation that usually follows in the aftermath of divorce. The magnitude of the current crisis is rooted, in part, to the lack of preparedness for marriage. This is why Dr. Aneesah Nadir's book, *Before the Nikah* , is so important. Dr. Nadir not only provides critical insight into how one prepares himself or herself for marriage, she also provides deep insight into the qualities one should look for in a prospective mate. The value of Dr. Nadir's book is only enhanced by the fact that her research and advice is not just relevant for members of the African American Muslim community, although addressing the crisis there is her particular concern. The insights the book presents are relevant for all ages and communities, as well as for those who may have been formerly married. In essence, Dr. Nadir has written a rich, nuanced text that I am confident will be well received by the Muslim community and beyond. This book is must reading for those seeking to form a strong Muslim family, as well as for those already married."

Imam Zaid Shakir -
Muslim Alliance in North America

"Before she was Dr. Nadir she was the most caring, loving, concerned mother I could ask for. Over the decades I've witnessed her evolution into an institution in the American Muslim Community. Her community mobilization efforts are internationally known. As a founder/co-founder and executive of pivotal organizations such as Islamic Social Services Association, Inc., Al-Muminah, and the Family Place, she has put her theories to the test. Personally, I've benefited immensely from observing her management of projects and people over the years. It is so rare to have a community activist/leader as attentive to their family as they are to the constituents they publicly serve. However, this is my mother. She is authentically a social worker and advocate for healthy families whether it's popular or not. Whether she's being appropriately valued and compensated or not. This is because she's a visionary. She lives her mission and has over the years recruited others to join her efforts. Dr. Nadir continues to be an inspiration for generations of social service and mental health professionals who have studied her work. The insights in this book are powerful because they lay out a roadmap for developing healthy families which will in turn cultivate healthy individuals and a healthy society. *Before the Nikah* is a gateway to benefit from Dr. Nadir's decades of research and refined community practice. The healthy marriage movement owes her a great debt for documenting her methodology and sharing it with the world through the *Before the Nikah* Institute. As your son and student, I could not be prouder!"

Dahir Nasser,
Diversity, Equity & Inclusion Consultant
V.P Social Justice Division,
Dr. Aneesah Nadir & Associates, LLC

Before THE Nikah

Before The Nikah:
Proven Principles to Help Single Muslims
Choose Wisely and Build Strong Marriages

The material in this book is supplied for informational purposes only and is not meant to take the place of professional advice. As your individual situation is unique, if you have questions relevant to your personal finances you should consult with a trusted professional. While all the stories and anecdotes are based on the author's experience and conversations, some of the names and identifying details of the persons involved have been changed to disguise those persons' identity. Any resulting resemblance to persons alive or dead is entirely coincidental and unintentional.

Published in the United States by Book Power Publishing, an imprint of Niyah Press, Detroit, Michigan.
www.bookpowerpublishing.com

Contact the author at: draneesah@gmail.com

First Edition
PRINTED IN THE UNITED STATES OF AMERICA.

ISBN: 978-1-945873-47-8

Contents

Part One

Note To Reader

The information contained in this book does not replace therapeutic or legal advice. The information provided in this book is not a replacement for the therapeutic relationship in psychotherapy, the coaching relationship or the legal relationship with your attorney. It is intended as general educational information. Any reliance on the information herein is at your sole discretion. You are encouraged to speak with your therapist, coach, or attorney for understanding on how the information specifically applies to you. Additionally, you are encouraged to consult with your religious leader or clergy on religious matters if you walk a particular spiritual path or adhere to a particular school of thought.

The stories shared here are for illustrative purposes only. Other than celebrities, the names and personally identifying characteristics have been changed. Any resemblance you see to yourself or someone you know is simply coincidental but a testament to how real life can get for more people than you think.

Dedication

To those
praying for a loving, compassionate,
fulfilling, and peaceful married life
May you be blessed to wisely choose your soulmate
May your caring and commitment
for each other blossom
May you and your family enjoy a
society full of tranquility, love and mercy

DR. P. ANEESAH NADIR

Before THE *Nikah*

Proven Principles to Help Single Muslims Choose Wisely and Build Strong Marriages

BOOK POWER PUBLISHING

Detroit, Michigan

Abbreviations

pbuh - Peace be upon him, used after Prophet Muhammad's name

Ra - From the Arabic radi Allahu 'anuhu or anhaa, which means may Allah be pleased with him or her, used after mentioning the name of the Prophet's companions

swt - From the Arabic subhanahu wa ta'aala, which means may He be glorified and exalted

Foreword

For decades, the award-winning Dr. Aneesah Nadir has gone against the grain to courageously declare that marriage preparation begins at day one! This comes from her deep faith, genuine love for community, and from being a social work practitioner for over 40 years. She has worked with teenagers and military families. She has practiced in hospital settings and group homes, in government agencies and in private practice. Dr. Nadir has published multiple articles for academia and popular magazines, was a columnist for a newspaper, co-authored multiple book chapters, and her work is regularly referenced in social work courses throughout the country. I refer to her as the Reverend of Social Work not only because she holds a bachelor's, master's, and Ph.D. in it; not only because she was a professor of social work at Arizona State University for almost 20 years; but, because she exudes social work. She truly loves seeing the system of society healthy for all its inhabitants from the youth to the elders, men and women, wealthy and financially struggling, and people of all ethnicities! She knows that a healthy marriage is a critical foundation to that and she has the receipts to prove it.

I love that Dr. Nadir visualizes a bigger picture and invites others in. She was blessed with the gift to see that the day you are born, your marriage path is charted. How your parents showed love to one another, how they showed love to you, how your family expressed empathy, how you learned to communicate your emotions, if you were punished when expressing yourself, or your working knowledge of the married life of Prophet Muhammad (pbuh) all impact how you show up looking to get married or starting an eventual marriage. It is this unique vision and perspective that she generously and unapologetically shares with local, national, and international communities and has been for decades.

This epic year has taught us that our home life matters. This year put an illuminating spotlight front and center on the relationship choices we made or were born into. For some, that spotlight felt like the gentle warmth of sun on your face after a chilly day. For others, it felt piercing hot like a laser beam. Hunkering down and sheltering in place tested even the best of relationships. The ones who were healthy used their established positive communication style to create new schedules, constructively share grievances and pull together as a team to work out solutions. It was stressful but they knew they were in it together and shared laptops so each could catch their zoom meetings. They called in a family member they mutually liked to help alleviate the round the clock childcare that was now needed. They budgeted for contactless food delivery so the one who usually cooked had some relief. Dad was called to wipe more toddlers' bums and change diapers while Mom made lesson plans for the kids. Finally at night when the phones stopped binging and ringing, and while they Netflix and chill, they realize they do not want to go through this with anyone else. They were happy and blessed they had chosen wisely, those years or months before, to be in a marriage with this person.

As an attorney, most people come to me when something bad has happened. Although I actively advocate against that strategy, I heard of many cases to the alternative. My colleagues and I saw that sheltering in place was a pressure cooker that accelerated the expiration date of many marriages. For other marriages that were teetering on the edge, Covid19 was the proverbial straw that broke the camel's back. These couples may have already realized that they did not choose wisely, but could tolerate their situation because they did not have to interact much. He worked all day. She worked all day. By the time they all connected at night, focusing on the kids for a couple of hours before bedtime was the buffer. This allowed them to not have to focus on the fact that they barely like each other, cannot communicate without feeling irritated about the other, have little in common, and if they were not married would probably not even choose to be friends. I heard multiple cases of one spouse hiding or taking the other spouse's portion of the stimulus check. I heard cases of emotional abuse that once were passed off as just snide remarks. I heard cases of physical violence and abuse.

So, now, they are heading for a marriage dissolution or divorce. While divorce is one of the hardest, emotionally draining, and expensive challenges someone could ever go through, I have never been one to be opposed to divorce because I found that many of the marriages that dissolve were not well suited matches in the first place. They were round pegs trying to fit into square holes and the divorce was the most merciful thing to do. Sometimes, though, there were couples that were great matches, but they did not have the tools earlier to give themselves the best shot. They did not know how to avoid a conflict from getting so far out of hand that it became irreconcilable. That is why this book, Before the Nikah, is so necessary.

This book takes the best and boldest approach I have ever seen—that is to help singles to choose wisely in the first place. Many books and courses on marriage start too late in my opinion. They are working with a couple who has already decided they want to get married. Often, the couple has succumbed to confirmation bias and as such is not truly open to advice. At this point they are bent on getting to the wedding day at all costs. This book can still be quite worthwhile for people already engaged or married if they stay receptive to learning and growing. But, that is not the savviest approach! This book helps you prevent going down the road that can cause unimaginable pain.

Dr. Nadir's excellence in social work has been awarded by local and national organizations including Social Worker of the Year by the National Association of Social Workers Arizona Chapter. She has received lifetime achievement awards from the Council on American Islamic Relations Arizona Chapter and the Islamic Society of North America. This year, her social entrepreneurism was also recognized when she was named 2021 Business Woman of the Year by the Tempe Chamber of Commerce, one of the oldest chambers of commerce in the United States. Her impact on the community was cited as a reason she was chosen for this honor.

Any student of Dr. Nadir can verify that healthy communities and healthy marriages are not a fad for her. I have been fortunate to have a front row seat to Dr. Aneesah Nadir. I have looked up to her my whole life and her example informed my community activism as a youth through my career path to becoming an attorney. From her I learned that the fight for social justice is not relegated to the streets but also justice must be had in the homes. For a good portion of my life, I am honored to say we have been co-conspirators in various projects serving the community. But, my biggest honor is that she is also my mother for whom I have deep respect. Her love for the youth of the community and her vision for all always astounded me. She started a youth group before my brothers and I were even old enough to join it and continued as its advisor long after we aged out. I also witnessed her develop the course *Before the Nikah* long before we were of marrying age. She continued to hone it and refine it over the years staying up to date on the trends and changing times because she truly believes people deserve a shot at having peaceful loving lives. So, I was blessed to grow up under the tutelage of Dr. Aneesah Nadir and her teachings. Alhumdulilah, this has helped me to prevent my heartbreaks from compounding into irreversible catastrophes!

I'm so thrilled that Dr. Aneesah Nadir is finally putting her wisdom and method for marriage preparation in a digestible book making it accessible to people for all time and in all places. To maximize its effects, this book is best as a companion to Dr. Nadir's *Before the Nikah Marriage Preparation Course*. However, you will gain considerable knowledge and skills even if you use a self-guided approach and sincerely engage in the "take action" activities.

My prayer is that as our community reads this thought-provoking book and applies the principles from it we will see a sizeable shift in the Muslim community with more people engaging in deeper introspection, skill building, and honesty prior to getting married so that the marriages that occur don't just last longer but that they are healthier. We will also see a seismic decrease in the proliferation of abuse in marriages as couples who have this knowledge can exit toxic situations sooner rather than later and ideally avoid them all together. Also, we will see people becoming more legally savvy as they enter marriage so they can avoid the messy divorces or if they do decide to dissolve can have a divorce with ihsan or dignity.   While geared toward Muslims, I recommend people of all faiths or non-faiths seeking a healthy marriage or a proponent for healthy families to read this book and apply the principles. This is a movement we should all be a part of. Many people say, "you never know how marriage is until you do it" or "there isn't a book on how to do this." Well, there is a book and *Before the Nikah* is it!

Zarinah Nadir
Attorney at Law
Author of Legally Savvy

Introduction

Perhaps you are among the skeptical who just don't see a need to spend time or money learning to prevent things from happening that aren't broken. You may be among those who believe that a marriage preparation course is not necessary. Perhaps you believe there is nothing in your religious tradition that obligates single people to engage in a course of study before marriage.

You may be the kind of person who must learn by personal experience. You may be the one that doesn't use a map or stop to get clear directions because you'll just find your own way and follow your nose. *If it ain't broken, don't fix it* and other euphemisms have gotten you into trouble, this book is not for you, at least not right now. Perhaps after you have tried it your way, you will come back to read this book.

Perhaps you picked up this book and said to yourself, "Before I even think of getting married, I better learn what it means to be married." Perhaps you received it as a gift from family or friends who have said there is important information to learn before you get married.

Perhaps you have decided since your first relationship or marriage was not what you hoped for you should learn some things to help you improve and grow so the next time around will be the loving fulfilling relationship you hoped for.

Perhaps you are convinced that it is important to learn about marriage and prepare yourself before you get married. Even though most folks spend more time planning their wedding than they spend on their marriage, you believe marriage is a Big Deal! If you believe marriage is not to be entered into casually or taken lightly and you want to learn how to choose wisely, *Before the Nikah* is for you!

This is a book of key skills, essential issues, and core principles you should consider and keep in mind before you begin the matrimonial process and sign the nikah marriage contract. It is a book for single men and women before they start the matrimonial search process, through meeting prospects for marriage, through becoming engaged, and through their marriage and wedding day. It is for newlyweds and those who are divorced. This book is written with a focus on Muslims in the U.S. but will also be beneficial for those in other western countries. While I have focused on Muslims in hopes of adding to the marriage material for the American Muslim community, the key principles and lessons are a benefit for those other faith, non faith and religious traditions. Consider the focus on the Muslims and the vignettes used as a kind of case study. Then think of your own faith tradition, terms and scriptural text, and exchange Islamic terms for terms you might use in your faith or traditional practices. The overarching message is that there are lessons to be learned and principles you want to consider and steps you want to take before you decide to marry or decide on the person you hope will be your lifelong partner. Being proactive and engaging in a marriage preparation course and a vetting process with the intention of taking steps to choose wisely, will help as you look for your spouse or lifelong partner to be compatible with you.

Why this book?

So why did I write this book and why am I so passionate about this sub-ject? I wrote this book because of what I saw between my parents when I was a child, what I experienced in my own married life, what I witnessed in the married lives of those close to me and, what I assessed profession-ally in clients' marriages over the past 40 years. I also wrote it because of what I saw as preventable marriage problems. The reality of the 50 percent divorce rate in society and the approximately 33 percent rate of divorce among Muslims in North America, according to sociologist Ilyas Ba-Yunus, affirms the need for this book. I have seen the impact of toxic marital relationships and bad divorce on children, the wife, the husband, extended family, and the community.

I have worked with adults who were in relationship trouble, or their marriage was on the brink of dissolution, who faced challenges that might have been addressed before or early in their marriage. The root of many relationships gone wrong has to do with people marrying without any real knowledge or understanding of what marriage involves and what it takes to make a healthy relationship, as well as the selection of a compatible spouse. Recently, I was speaking with a group of my sister friends about what we learned about marriage as young women. They were 10 to15 years older than me and reflected on learning home-making and home economics skills but little if anything about how to choose a compatible spouse or relationship building skills.

The lack of good communication skills is another key factor which leads to the breakdown of a relationship. Communication skills can be learned and developed. Too often couples form a relationship with a host of expectations about marriage and their prospective spouse that they never really talked about - unexpressed expectations. Too often people are forming a marital relationship when they do not know themselves and they have not taken time to get to really know the person they intend to have this lifelong relationship with and eventually raise children with.

Being Single. The Struggle is real.

Before the Nikah is a book for the diverse single Muslim community in the U.S., Canada, and other Western countries. It is also beneficial for singles of other faith traditions who can relate to the messages conveyed here. Having been single, married, single, divorced, and remarried for 40 years; I can relate to the different aspects of singlehood and married life. I have also had entre, as a parent of young adults, as a youth group and MSA (Muslim Student Association) advisor and close friends with single and divorced people in the 20 to50 age range. Many are still in the search and haven't given up the search while others have become disheartened about the future prospects. I have seen different sides and aspects of being single. I empathize and recognize that the struggle is real.

Back in the early 90s, I started out by dipping my toe in the matchmaking arena. A close friend and colleague and I started a matchmaking program but we realized very quickly that the issues were very complex. Security was a challenge and ensuring honesty by applicants required so much more than we knew and was nearly impossible. So we decided to leave that arena, although we still believe helping singles find their match is very important.

I also recognized that one of the issues—even if they were matched with someone who was honest—was the lack of knowledge about marriage, particularly marriage in Islam, communication and relationship skills as well as conflict resolution and problem solving skills. So, I decided to focus on premarital education and marriage preparation before people begin the search, early on in their search, or as newlyweds.

I have found that Muslim singles are not a monolithic group. There are young adults who haven't even started looking, haven't begun their matrimonial search. There are those who have been searching for some time and are now in their 40s and 50s but have never been married even though they wanted to be. There are those who have been married and are now divorced or widowed. For some the divorce was amicable, but for many it was traumatic and emotionally devastating.

Among those singles—who were married before—there are those who don't see themselves getting married again. The trauma is too much to risk reliving. Some are still grieving the loss of their first marriage and their second marriage. So many had high hopes for their married life that did not live up to their expectations. They hoped it would be a storybook with their meeting, courtship, and marriage starting happily *ever after*. Others looked forward to living the core values of marriage in Islam—love, compassion, and tranquility—but their hopes were dashed when they found the person they married was not interested in nor did they adhere to Islamic beliefs and lifestyle. So many married without knowledge of marriage according to Islam, without basic communication and relationship skills, and without someone compatible and well-suited for them. Others didn't know how to vet or have support through the vetting process and married someone who lied to them and broke their heart. Still others have decided that they are Muslim and happily single with no plans to get in the matrimonial search. They understand that marriage is part of the traditions of the Prophet ☐, but they have decided they do better as a single person. Muslim singles are American born; they are converts, children and grandchildren of converts, immigrants and refugees. They are from different racial, cultural, and ethnic groups. They have grown up practicing Islam, as well as the culturalized traditions of Islam as practiced by their group. Others have converted to Islam from various cultures, racial, and ethnic groups. They range in age from younger to older and face an assortment of challenges.

One challenge that I hear often is the differing views they have from their parents. Many are concerned that their parents' views about the person they should marry is very different from their own. Parents want them to marry someone from the same culture, tribe, race, or group as they belong to. Our young singles cave in out of respect for their parents and a desire to please them, or they continue to see a person that would not be approved of, without their parents knowledge causing conflict and feelings of guilt. Their parents may have these preferences so that they can communicate and enjoy religious and cultural traditions together. The children, born and raised in the U.S. or Canada, may have never lived in their parents' home country, and sometimes feel they would not be compatible with someone from "back home".

Another challenge is that the Muslim population in the U. S. is very small. In larger urban areas there are larger populations of Muslims however, according to a Washington Post article, Muslims represent no more than 2 percent of the U.S. population, "so finding a mate is a bit like looking for a needle in a haystack." This is especially difficult in certain parts of the country. It's really hard for single U.S. Muslims to meet. Forty years ago we saw the stark difference when we moved from New York City to Phoenix, where African Americans were only 5 percent of the Arizona population and the Muslim community was even smaller than that. Black American Muslims are still a small percentage of the Arizona population today.

And there simply are a lot more single women than single men in society so Muslim men see themselves as having many more options and various backgrounds to select from including Muslim women, women of the Abrahamic traditions and for some women of other faith and non faith traditions as part of their prospective pool. According to Genevieve Glatsky, author of South Philadelphia Mosque takes on matchmaking of Black Muslim women, finds "Muslims concerned about what they consider to be an epidemic of educated, professional women older than 30 struggling to find suitable matches among Muslim men, who are often less bound by a biological clock and societal expectations, and more likely than Muslim women to marry younger and outside their culture or religion."

Black Muslim women experience additional challenges as they are increasingly educated, and professional women who find it difficult to meet men with similar educational and socio-economic backgrounds.

"Just 49 percent of college-educated black women marry well-educated men (i.e, with at least some post-secondary education), compared to 84 percent of college-educated white women according to an analysis by Yale sociologist Vida Maralani. According to a 2015 Brookings

Institution report, 'black women have the lowest rates of 'marrying out' across racial lines.'" (Glatsky, 2017)

Those who are still looking and hoping to marry someone compatible are discouraged by the matrimonial search process. Whether it be parents and friends arranging a match, amateur or professional matchmakers, or online matrimonial sites.

Muslim singles, like other groups, are discouraged by the pool and the difficulty they have finding Muslims who are kind, sincere, honest, empathetic, goal oriented, open to blended family structures,have a balanced perspective of Islam, and are truly practicing the essence and heart of Islam.

Zarinah El-Amin summarizes 8 reasons being a young single Muslim is difficult in her book *Jihad of the Soul.* She concluded that being young, Muslim, and single isn't easy. The challenge of navigating family expectations, Islamic traditions and practices , popular culture, physical desires, and loneliness, in a community that does not facilitate positive permissible interaction between young men and women who want to marry, only adds to the difficulty Muslim singles face. It is clear the struggle is real. Single Muslims, their families, and community have considerable work to do to ease the challenges for the current and future generations, as well as those who are older and still have the hope of a healthy Muslim marriage.

The search is difficult and Muslims, like other groups, are marrying with little or no education about marriage and relationships. They spend more time on the search and wedding preparation phase than on the premarital education and marriage preparation phase. They also spend little time learning how to make a wise selection. This is what the *Before the Nikah* book and course are all about.

Part One

Chapter 1

PREVENTION

Among the common marriage problems are financial issues, lack of communication or poor communication skills, infidelity, and domestic abuse. **Having a proactive prevention-oriented mindset is a core *Before the Nikah* principle and a key to a healthy marriage.**

What is prevention and why is it important for a healthy marriage? Throughout my years as a social worker and family life educator working with young people and families, I have found that our society and community tend to operate from a reactive, treatment-based perspective rather than a proactive, preventive-based perspective. We tend to work to fix that which is broken and in ill-repair rather than prevent problems in the first place. We tend to be short-sighted rather than taking the long view. I support therapy and treatment and advocate for treatment services and programs. However, treatment is more expensive than prevention, and people rarely pay for services or fund programs that prevent problems because the return on investment takes longer to see. How can you see if your strategy worked on something that isn't broken? Many believe in the adage, "If it ain't broke don't fix it." While fewer believe in the saying, "An ounce of prevention is worth a pound of cure." Prophet Muhammad's saying (pbuh), "Tie your camel and rely on Allah," is a reminder of the importance of prevention in Islam, as well as the importance of using all resources available to us to prevent and solve problems, as we trust Allah for the outcome. Still, many of us are not proactive or preventative when it comes to marriage.

> *In a hadith of Prophet Muhammad, (pbuh) Anas ibn Malik reported: A man said, "O Messenger of Allah, should I tie my camel and trust in Allah, or should I leave her untied and trust in Allah?" The Prophet, peace and blessings be upon him, said, "Tie her and trust in Allah. " (Sunan al-Tirmidhi 2517)*

The literature describes three categories of prevention: primary, secondary, and tertiary (Wolfe and Jaffe, 1999). The three levels are also known as primary prevention, early intervention, and treatment. Primary prevention focuses on addressing a problem before it happens. For example, lock your car, your house, and set the alarm system before someone attempts to steal it or break in. Get your mammogram, engage in regular checkups, good nutrition, drink plenty of water, sleep, and exercise before you get sick. Secondary prevention's goal is to decrease the frequency of a problem by minimizing or reducing its severity and the continuation of its early signs. In this level of prevention, when we experience the first signs of the sniffles or a cough, we pump up the Vitamin C, get out the humidifier, go to bed early before these symptoms turn into the flu, bronchitis, or worse yet, pneumonia. In the treatment phase we are looking at being admitted to the hospital Intensive Care Unit for pneumonia, or dialysis treatment because of out of control diabetes, or chemotherapy/radiation for cancer. This is the level we are much more familiar with. As a society and a community, we tend to focus on fixing broken issues rather than prevention of problems before they occur.

Before the Nikah is a primary prevention-based premarital course taken before you begin your matrimonial search. Even better, you are one or more years away from beginning the process of meeting potential prospects. It is early intervention before you're engaged or newly married. This is the stage at which you want to learn some things that will help prevent you from marrying the wrong person or going down a path that could lead to a toxic relationship. Learning information about what to look for and look out for, the vetting process, as well as gaining relationship-building skills before you start looking, are important steps toward a healthy marriage.

You may have areas you need to work on. Identifying them early on can avoid heartache for you and your prospective spouse. We shouldn't practice on people. The earlier we fine-tune our character and develop healthy relationship skills, the more likely we are to have a healthy marriage.

Chapter 2

PREMARITAL EDUCATION AND MARRIAGE PREPARATION

Most people spend more time planning their wedding day than their married life. Learning key values and core principles you should know before marriage and continuing your education during the relationship, demonstrates the value and priority you place on your union and family. So many think it is good enough to learn about marriage on the job. Well, get married and just dive right in and take it as it comes is one view. You will learn a lot, but there are essentials you will want to learn before you begin the matrimonial process to prevent a toxic future marriage.

So, what is marriage preparation, and how important is it before you marry? Simply put, marriage preparation is the opportunity to learn about marriage, what causes problems within it, as well as what makes a healthy union. Also referred to as premarital education, according to Hawkins and Clyde (2018), it is an "education program offered to couples preparing for or seriously considering marriage. An effective premarital education program helps prospective or engaged couples evaluate their relationship prior to marriage by covering potentially problematic areas and providing preventive skills training to help couples improve their relationship and reduce the risk of divorce." Most folks learn marriage on the job and discover what marriage is along the way. However, in conversations about marriage with friends, many often say in hindsight, they wish they had known so much more before they got married. Participating in a premarital course is a forum to gain the knowledge we need before we marry.

Programs and efforts to prepare people for marriage date back to the 1930s. Marriage preparation began with clergy, who are the primary providers of premarital education in the U.S. (Killawi, et al, 2017; Murray, 2005).

Participants are generally engaged couples referred by the church to the clergy or pastoral counselor. Most couples in the United States do not participate in marriage preparation programs (Silliman & Schumm, 2000). Those who do, seek premarital education through a religious institution (Glenn, 2005).

Premarital education and marriage preparation programs are part of a continuum of marriage education programs and services geared for couples. The continuum ranges from premarital education and premarital counseling to marriage education, marriage enrichment, and marriage counseling or therapy. They include opportunities to increase couple awareness of marital challenges and strategies to address them, relationship building skills, couples retreats, mentorship with veteran married couples, and a variety of activities. The movie *Licensed to Wed* starring Robin Williams, provides a Hollywood look at a premarital course for couple Sadie and Ben who decided to marry at her church, St Augustine.

Among U.S. Muslims, standardized Islamically based curriculums for premarital education are limited. The premarital education that is available is primarily provided by imams for engaged couples and is limited in scope. They are brief and focused largely on the marriage contract and on religiously based rights and responsibilities. There are mosques and Islamic centers that require couples to participate in marriage preparation, however, they are limited (Killawi, et al, 2017). Almost half of participants in the Killawi, et al., 2017 study believed couples should be required to participate in premarital counseling or some type of premarital education.

There is certainly a need for premarital education for couples and continuing marriage education, enrichment, and counseling throughout the marriage. However, I strongly recommend you begin premarital education before you identify someone you want to marry. I strongly recommend high school students begin to learn relationship skills and lessons from the Prophet's example, peace be upon him, in preparation for future marriage and family life. I also strongly encourage premarital education for those of any age who are single, never married and those who have been previously married before they remarry. **Premarital education and marriage preparation for those who are single and not engaged is a core *Before the Nikah* principle.** In addition to relationship-building skills, information about Islamic marital rights and responsibilities, **learning how to utilize the vetting process, and the importance of thorough background checks are also core *Before the Nikah* principles.**

For this book, premarital education and marriage preparation are defined as education about yourself, your prospective spouse, what makes a healthy marriage, the vetting process, and relationship-building skills. While most premarital education programs tend to be for engaged couples, this book's focus is on education for single men and women. Parents are encouraged to support opportunities for their youth and young adults to participate in courses, workshops, and programs that will prepare them with healthy marriage and relationship skills way before they meet the person they may want to marry. Many of the skills pertain to having healthy relationships in general, as with parents, siblings, friends, and coworkers. The sooner one can begin the education process the better. And as you mature, take opportunities for continuing marriage education, over time. The more those who engage in marriage preparation see it as a normal part of young adult and adult development, the more benefits they will receive from it. The benefits of participation in premarital education with the *Before the Nikah* course are the ability to learn and apply what you learn over twelve sessions, two hours per week; unlike the three to six sessions provided by many premarital courses.

Chapter 3

Informed Consent, People Don't Always Tell the Truth

Another key *Before the Nikah* principle is Informed Consent. We believe that anyone desiring to marry has a right and a responsibility to know what they are getting into. Your job in the search process is to do your due diligence, as well as expect the other person to be honest and not hide information that will impact your future married life. This is a key aspect of the vetting process, truly getting to know your prospective spouse and giving the process time to reveal what is important for you to know. You have a right and a responsibility to know about your prospective spouse's background even if you decide to marry them with their challenged past. With knowledge, you can weigh the benefits and the challenges against the core values of a healthy marriage and make an informed decision. You can weigh the potential consequences of your decision. Unfortunately, many people hide their reality for fear the other person will not marry them if they are honest and forthright. You may decide you want to marry despite the health, legal, or other challenges your prospective spouse has, but you should know so you can make an informed decision to marry or not. That is your choice. You should not wake the morning after the wedding to learn your spouse is not who they say they are. You should know during the vetting and courtship phase that your prospective is facing immigration challenges or needs help being sponsored for her green card, is in credit card debt, has a sexually transmitted disease, has a child from a previous relationship, is in deportation proceedings, is formerly incarcerated, or doesn't plan to live in the U.S. when married.

So, give it time. Plan to get to know each other throughout various experiences and challenges that life presents. Use the proprietary *Before the Nikah Vetting Process.* Require honesty of yourself and others. Be kind and respectful. Demonstrate good manners and vet for the same. Alhamdulilah there are good people with good hearts and good intentions that are true and honorable in this world and want to marry and be a good, kind spouse. It is also important not to be naive and to recognize that in this world there are people who lie, hide the truth, have ulterior motives, are hypocrites, and some who are wolves in sheep's clothing. The reality that there are those who are not honest is often difficult to accept; however, Allah tells us in various places in the Qur'an such as Surah Al-Baqara (2:1-20) and Surah Maun (107: 1-7) that such people exist and that we should beware.

> *Consider the story of Asma. Asma was 19 years old, a recent high school graduate on the way to undergrad school with aspirations to become an attorney. She had strong connections in her community and was well liked. One day Khalid came to town. It is not clear how he came to know of Asma; however, before her friends and family knew anything he had asked her parents to marry her. The brief inquiries about his background seemed to indicate he was nice and was considerate of his family, especially his sisters. He was not well-known but seemed nice enough. It*

seemed like a love story. Rather quickly, they were married. And before anyone knew anything, Asma was gone to her new home in her new city with someone neither she nor her family really knew. Not too long after, Asma learned that she was one of her husband's three wives. He was part of a community that practiced polygny but had not revealed that to her family. He was not honest about his marital situation and her family had not conducted a thorough background check and engaged in a thorough vetting. Asma was married and became one of three sister wives without her knowledge or consent. She may still have decided Khalid was the one for her, but she was not given an opportunity to make a knowledgeable, informed choice.

Chapter 4

KNOW THYSELF AND TO THINE OWNSELF BE TRUE

Knowing yourself and being honest with yourself about who you are is a core *Before the Nikah* principle.

Getting to know yourself takes time and is an ongoing process as you mature and engage in personal development. It is not a brief one-hour activity. This is a process that requires introspection over time. When you don't know yourself, it is difficult to determine the kind of person who will be compatible with you.

There are various tools that can be used to assist you in getting to know yourself. Some of the personal assessment tools that you can use include:

- The **Myers Briggs Type Indicator** which provides insight about differing personality types.

- Gary Chapman's **Five Love Languages Quiz** gives us a clue about how we express and receive love; that is how we love to be loved.
- **ACEs Quiz** identifies the adverse childhood experiences that have put many of us at risk during childhood. They are traumatic experiences we had before adulthood that may impact the person we are physically, psychologically, and emotionally as adults. School psychologist, Latisha Ojuriye reminds us that the ACEs Quiz gives us insight into our experiences, so that we can address them before marriage and during the various phases of our married lives.

There are a variety of communication style quizzes. They help you assess your personal communication style. Is your style more passive, aggressive, passive-aggressive, or assertive? It will be important to know your style and your prospective spouse's style to determine communication compatibility.

Journaling about different periods of your life like childhood memories, high school, as well as different aspects of your life like your spiritual life, your family, community, business, personal life may give clues about yourself. Whichever tools you choose, be honest with yourself.

As you conduct your personal self-assessment, you will also want to consider what characteristics you want in your future spouse and what characteristics you think will be compatible with you as you get to know yourself. Most of us spend little or no time getting to know who we are. One of the first things I ask someone looking to get married is, "Tell me about yourself." I also ask about their vision for their marriage and family and what they are looking for in their future spouse. Most have little to share because they haven't spent much time getting to know themselves. Their vision for their future is often very shallow because they have not thought much about it. They say things like, "I want a good Muslim and kids." Well, good is relative and kids could mean 1 to 10 kids, even more. Getting to know oneself is essential. It is crucial that time is spent getting to know what you bring to the table, the kind of person you are looking for, and who you want to be.

Questions to ask yourself are:

- What do I value in life—my belief in Allah, my family, education, money, helping people, honesty? What is my temperament—easy going, harsh, or a bit of both? What makes me angry? How do I handle anger? And stress? How is my health? My mental health?
- What do I want out of life—my goals and dreams? What do I imagine marriage to be? What are my hopes and dreams for my marriage, my children, my family?

Truthfully, one is not ready for marriage until you have taken time to get to know yourself. And as we do, we should resolve to be honest about the person who we discover we are, including our weaknesses, strengths, and areas for improvement.

I have taken opportunities for personal and professional assessment. Professionally, I believe that I am a social worker at my core no matter what else I do as a business woman or entrepreneur. Social work is at my core. As I looked at characteristics, my personal characteristics, I considered areas I wanted to improve. I decided I wanted to work on being more generous and more tender. Over time, I realized some of my experiences had caused me to be tougher than I wanted to be. I also determined I wanted to learn to truly trust in Allah and constantly affirm that He has my back. Currently, I am working on seeing the world as spacious and realizing there are many options for places I may want to live or spend time in the world. I tend to be a stay-put, settled person, but I am also realizing that I

*may need to step out of my comfort zone to experience more
of what the world has to offer.*

Even learning these aspects of my more mature self are key to my continued growth and self-improvement and to improving my relationships with my family. There is truly room for growth as I continue to get to know myself.

Starting your self analysis now, continuing to get to know yourself and working on you will be essential as you identify characteristics that will be the best fit for you and your future spouse. Be true to who you are and the type of person with whom you will be compatible.

Someone who is self-centered and harsh may not be ready for marriage. A person at this place in life will need to spend time working on personal development and learning to be more giving and easygoing. It will be important to honestly convey this aspect of yourself with your Marriage Success Team (MST), which we discuss later, your support system, your parents, or wali as they assist you in your search for a prospective spouse who is compatible. They need to know how you see yourself and you want to know how they see you.

Most of us are not ready for marriage until we are ready to be honest with ourselves and our prospective spouse. The reality is too many of us do not know ourselves. And too many of us do not tell the truth about who we are, if we do know ourselves.

Sadly, many people don't tell the truth

It pains me to say that so many of the people getting married are people who don't know themselves, aren't true to themselves and aren't true to the person they are discussing possibilities of marriage with. Not only aren't they true but many downright lie. But why? Some are not honest because they know who they are and share who they think the other person wants them to be. They don't want the other person to know the person they are because they are pretty sure the other person will not want to marry them. Others lie because they intentionally want to make themselves look like someone they are not. Some are exploiters and con artists and see you as a means to their ends. No matter how you slice it, intentionally lying about yourself to yourself, to your prospective spouse, not sharing the real you, including your strengths and your challenges, or sharing things about yourself that aren't true will not be helpful in preparing for a healthy marriage. In some cases, it can be criminal. Let us remember that, in any case, Allah sees us, even if people don't.

Most people want to put themselves in the best light. We do not want our prospective spouse to see us the way we look first thing in the morning with bad breath and our hair all over the place. If more people took time to get to know themselves, were honest with themselves and their prospective spouse, and more people seriously took time to conduct a background check and consult with their parents, wali, and support system; more couples would be ready to begin a healthy marriage.

Be honest and truthful. We all have shortcomings we need to work on, weak areas we want to improve on, or realize we should work on, to better ourselves. This is an opportunity to engage in personal, professional, and spiritual self-development to become our best selves. Look for prospects who are likewise working on getting to truly know themselves and engage in personal and spiritual self-development. Commit to having honest truthful conversations with your prospective spouse and a premarital therapist or marriage coach about who you both are and whether you are ready for marriage, especially marriage with each other.

Listen for signs that the prospective spouse is being honest. Vague or grandiose answers are a red flag. Constantly quoting ahadith but not sharing how that personally applies to them is problematic.

Consider the story of Aliya. Aliya was talking to Brother Abraham. Whenever she asked him about his view on children he said, "God says they are blessings." When she asked him about why he wanted to be married, he said,"God says to get married if you are able." And when she asked if he wanted his mother to live with them eventually, he said, "Heaven is at the mother's feet." Quoting hadith and verses from Qur'an are one thing, however having an honest conversation about how the verses and hadith apply to you and will play out in your married life is another important aspect of the process of getting to know each other.

TAKE ACTION

Who Am I? My Personal Self-Assessment

Use this space to begin to journal about yourself. Describe yourself.

Who are you?

What cultural, racial, language, faith, career community do you identify with?

What is important to you?

What are your key values?

What are your successes?

What have been your challenges?

What are your goals and dreams for your future?

Where do you see yourself and your family in 5 years, 10 years, 20 years, inshaAllah? How do you see yourself?

What is your love language?

What is your communication style?

How is your physical and mental health?

What is your temperament?

Who are the key people in your life? Family? Friends?

What is your relationship with Islam? Allah? The Prophet Muhammad? The Muslim community? The faith community? Your social media community?

The community in which you live? Your professional community? Your society? Global Society?

What are your strengths? What are things about yourself you want to work on or improve?

Do you have a cause that is important to you? If so, briefly discuss. For example, Racial justice, global warming, animal rights, etc.

____

____

____

____

____

____

____

____

____

Chapter 5

KEYS TO A
HEALTHY MARRIAGE
IN ISLAM

Understanding the verses in Qur'an and examples from the life of Prophet Muhammad are core *Before the Nikah* principles.

So, what is a healthy marriage in Islam? In Qur'an Surah Al-Rum (30: 21), Allah reminds us that spouses were created from the same origin. A healthy marriage is one in which Allah has placed love (muwada) and mercy or compassion (rahmah) between spouses so that they find peace and tranquility (sakinah) in their relationship. Abugidieri and Magid describe the Qur'anic model of a healthy marriage as including equality, love, mercy, and mutuality. The Qur'an (2:187) further refers to spouses as being garments for each other. Just as our clothes cover us, are protective, comfortable, warm, make us look good, feel good, and secure; so does a healthy marriage. Our clothing comes in different types of material. Just as you want your clothing to suit you, you want your spouse to be a good fit and suit you. What kind of garment do you want your spouse to reflect ? Do you want a garment of wool, silk, or cotton? You want a garment that fits well. You want a marriage that makes you feel protected, cared for, and covered. A healthy marriage in Islam is one that is full of love and compassion and is peaceful, not full of drama. It is a relationship that helps us grow in our understanding of ourselves and our relationship with Allah.

The Best Example

The divorce rate is an indicator of the example so many see of marriage. I did not have the best examples of a healthy marriage or relationship as my own parents had a troubled marriage. When my husband proposed I was reluctant to accept because of what I had experienced growing up. Fifty percent of marriages in America end in divorce and thirty-three percent of Muslim marriages in North America end in divorce. Therefore, many of us don't see examples of a healthy marriage in our lives. The good news is the Prophet Muhammad's (pbuh), marital life provides an example for us. Alhamdulillah, he is our best example, and we get to see how he and his wives related to each other. He, pbuh, was married to his wife Khadijah (ra) for 25 years. While she was alive, she was his only wife. The year of her passing was called the Year of Sorrow. Sometime after her passing, he married Sawdah, a widow with young children. His marriages solidified different aspects of the nascent community. We have stories of how he demonstrated what it means to be a good husband, father, stepfather, and grandfather. His married life taught us profound lessons 1400 years ago about different ways to demonstrate healthy marital relationships.

Prophet Muhammad and Khadijah: Theirs was a Love Story

The Prophet (pbuh), and Khadijah married when he was 25 and she was 40. Khadijah was considered Meccan royalty, the daughter of Khuwaylid ibn Asad, a leader of the Quraysh tribe in Mecca. She was like a princess, if they had them in that society at that time. She was a widow with children from her previous marriage and the owner of a big business in Mecca. In today's context she might be considered the Owner and Chief Executive Officer of an "Amazon" of her day and a single parent widow. She was looking for someone she could employ and trust with her caravan of merchandise. She and others observed young adult Muhammad's, pbuh, character and his behavior, which led her to decide he would make a good employee. He was an excellent employee and brought her significant return on her investment as her business grew under his management. He was not only good for her business but the feedback she received about his character and integrity also led her to see him as a good prospect for marriage. Khadijah proposed and he,(pbuh), accepted her proposal for marriage. They married and he managed her business. They had six children, two of which died as infants.

Today, women who were previously married, divorced, or widowed are often stigmatized. So many women are single because their prospects for remarriage are considered limited and these women are looked down upon. The marriage of Khadijah (ra) and Prophet Muhammad (pbuh), is an example of a blended family with her children from her previous marriages and their children. While this is rarely mentioned in the literature, I address it here to make us aware of this part of the sunnah, in hopes of reducing the stigma that so many widowed and divorced women and single parents face.

We also see from this example that Khadijah (ra) used an important vetting process; observation of his behavior and his character around people, how was his integrity and behavior in business and with money, as well as what people had to say about him (pbuh). She utilized her support system to help with the vetting. Through this vetting process she learned that he was a person of exemplary character. That led her to propose to him, which he accepted.

Khadijah (ra) and the Prophet (pbuh), were married for 25 years. During this time, she was his only wife. He loved and cared for her, her family, and her business. When the Angel Gabriel conveyed the message that he (pbuh) would be the next prophet, he was overcome, but she was there to comfort him and reassure him. She supported the Prophet (pbuh) and the early Muslim community with her reputation and her wealth. They loved and supported each other. Theirs is a beautiful love story. The year Khadijah (ra) and the Prophet's Uncle Abu Talib died is known as the Year of Sorrow for the Prophet (pbuh). It was a significantly depressing time, as he, pbuh, loved them both so much. He, pbuh, experienced grief and depression as a result of their passing. Allah comforted him.

His (pbuh) love for her continued even after her death, and he demonstrated how much he appreciated her and how grateful and proud he was of their relationship. He (pbuh) would continue to maintain warm memories of her throughout his life which he shared with those around him. He was deeply grateful that she had confidence in him (pbuh), was the first convert to Islam, and demonstrated her love, and used her wealth and resources to support the mission. He frequently visited her friends after she died in appreciation and memory of her.

Aisha (ra)

In the Prophet's marriage to Aisha, (ra) daughter of Abu Bakr, we saw his appreciation for her youth, his love and care for her, as well as his patience and playfulness with her. We saw them race each other and he would join her to watch entertainment. Their marriage strengthened the relationship between her father, Abu Bakr (ra) and the Prophet, pbuh. She was raised Muslim, while most of the companions of the Prophet pbuh, including Abu Bakr (ra), were converts to Islam. Aisha (ra) was recognized by her husband, the Prophet, pbuh, for her intelligence and scholarship. She is credited with narrating more than 2000 hadith, giving us insight into the Prophet's traditions about religion, family, community, and societal life.

So What is a Healthy Marriage?

The author of the *Muslim Marriage Guide*, Ruqqayah Waris, conveys the Prophet's (pbuh) respect for his wives' opinions, sensitivity for their feelings, and his respect for their intelligence and advice. He was a step-father to their children and an example of a loving, nurturing presence in his family and community.

So, what is a healthy marriage? A healthy marriage is one that characterizes the married life of the Prophet, (pbuh). It shows love, tenderness, patience, compassion, concern, and security. It is one that demonstrates peace and tranquility. It is one in which there is support and encouragement despite the adversity. It is one that demonstrates service to Allah and striving to get to Heaven.

So, what are keys to a healthy marriage? Allah outlines the core keys to a healthy marriage in Sura Rum (30:21). He tells us that they include having love for one another, being compassionate with one another, and maintaining peace and tranquility between each other. In Sura Al-Baqara (2:187), Allah says, as spouses we are garments for each other. These verses tell us that a healthy marriage in Islam is built on a foundation of love of God and a desire to please and serve Him. A healthy marriage is a union that demonstrates respect for each other, kindness towards one another, empathy, healthy mature emotional behavior, and the ability to communicate with each other lovingly and respectfully. It is also a marriage in which each person demonstrates good manners, a mutual concern, and a desire to do well with and for each other. A healthy marriage is not a toxic relationship with ongoing drama. In a healthy relationship both spouses feel safe. No one feels like they're walking on eggshells. No one feels like they must hide things. They feel like they have a relationship open to talk about their concerns and grow in a kind and loving way. That doesn't mean that there won't be disagreements, however in a healthy relationship they are opportunities to learn not to debase each other. We utilize healthy communication, mutual consultation, problem solving, and conflict resolution skills so that we can resolve and address our concerns in a loving way.

Before the Nikah prepares you for a healthy marriage. Starting your relationship with a spiritual connection to Allah and continuing to cultivate and grow your relationship with the Creator and each other is essential. Your relationship with Allah provides a solid foundation on which to build your relationship and receive guidance through the adversity that is inevitable in every union. So, as you get to know yourself be sure to get to know your Creator so that you have His guidance throughout every stage of the matrimonial process and the phases of your married life. Be sure to vet for a person who has taqwa and is committed to serving Allah.

TAKE ACTION

Qur'an Sura Al-Rum (30:21)

Qur'an Sura Al-Baqara (2:187)

"The Blessed Prophet and his Wives" in *The Muslim Marriage Guide* by Ruqaiyyah Waris Maqsood

Biographies of the Women Companions of the Holy Prophet by Maulana Saeed Ansari Nadvi et al.

The Qur'anic Model in *Before You Tie the Knot* by Salma Abugideiri and Mohamed Magid

Chapter 6

KEY SKILLS:
COMMUNICATION

Communication is a key skill you want to know before you begin exploring marriage prospects. Acquiring healthy communication skills is a key *Before the Nikah* principle. The ability to communicate is a key skill before and during marriage. Our ability to communicate our wants, needs, and expectations as well as listen to the wants and needs of our prospective spouse before and during marriage is key. It is also an essential part of the vetting process to truly get to know the person you are considering marrying. Communication problems are among the top challenges to a healthy marriage. The literature on marriage continues to point to the breakdown in communication.

Being able to communicate with your prospective spouse is key. Without healthy communication skills as a couple, you will likely experience ongoing conflict with one another.

Communication

When you think about communication what comes to mind? Talking, speaking with each other, listening to each other, feeling each other's energy. Communication is a two-way process. It's not one-way. It is not just talking with each other . We communicate messages verbally and non-verbally. We communicate with facial expressions, our body language, gestures, tone of voice, and speech patterns. Communication is about two parties being able to communicate with one another, to share ideas, thoughts, perspectives, discuss differences of opinion, and views. It is discussing important issues as well as trivial ones. It is shooting the breeze, laughing together, and reminiscing. Things that make communicating easy and difficult are also known as obstacles and facilitating factors.

Obstacles and facilitating factors

What are some of the obstacles and facilitating factors to good communication? Communication between those with whom you are intimately connected requires a willingness to communicate with each other, having a heart, empathy, care, and concern for each other. These will make your communication easier and more meaningful.

In today's fast paced life, good communication skills can help you express your desire to talk at times that better accommodate both of you and minimize the challenges of being on different schedules. This will address what might be considered a timing challenge. It's important to have your timing synchronized. If one person is exhausted from the day and the other person is energetic and ready to talk late at night, a smooth conversation may be challenging.

Speaking different languages may present barriers to positive communication. If you don't speak the same language, or even if you speak the same common language but it's not your native tongue, that could present a barrier. Use of different colloquial phrases may also affect how you communicate and how you understand each other.

> *Paula and Omar spoke English but his native language*
> *was Spanish. In marriage counseling they complained that*
> *the same conversation that would have probably taken an*

hour for people who have a common native language, took them five times as long and was difficult because they just really did not understand each other. She did not speak Spanish and he did not understand the American English language nuances and references she shared.

Basic respect for each other was also missing in communication between Paula and Omar. When you are communicating with one another you will want to demonstrate respect, appreciation, and value for one another such that you want to listen to what each other is saying. There are so many aspects to a healthy way of communicating, but the bottom line is caring for each other and appreciating each other in a way that enables you to communicate in a caring, loving, thoughtful, and respectful way.

What are factors that make our communication easier? Things that make communication easier and clearer include caring for one another, respect, and compassion. Good listening skills like being respectful, attentive, open to the other person, and attuned to each other's feelings facilitate communication. Being rested and limiting distractions also facilitate good communication.

Conversely, it is challenging to communicate if you have had a long day and you're tired and hungry. When you're tired, you are not able to think as clearly and be as patient. Feeling angry can be an obstacle to good communication. Feeling angry with the person you are communicating with makes it difficult to have a productive conversation and see each other's perspective. It is likely you do not even want to talk. Another obstacle is background noise, perhaps a TV in the background, children, or other family members talking or playing. This may also make it difficult to have good communication with one another. Speaking the same language and understanding cultural references make communication easier.

Communication with one another over social media is possible, but you can't really feel the energy in the same way that you can when you're face-to-face. You miss the nuances of the spoken word, like a tone of sarcasm, or humor. You miss facial expressions and body language. WhatsApp or text messaging across different time zones can really make it very difficult to communicate clearly and with sensitivity. Turning off your social media notifications and your cell phone can facilitate communication and demonstrate you are present and focused.

Communication Style

Since communication is such an important part of your relationship, it is critical before you get married to assess and discern your prospective spouse's communication style. Determine whether your communication styles are compatible. During your personal assessment you have given thought to what your communication style is.

There are 3-4 types of communication styles. Alvernia University identifies four types: passive, aggressive, passive-aggressive, and assertive. Stacy Kaiser provides an online Communication Style Quiz that delineates three communication styles as passive communicator, aggressive communicator, and dynamic communicator. In the premarital phase, it is important to determine your communication style and your prospecti. How do you feel when you communicate with each other? Do you both feel happy, resolved, and fulfilled or unheard, powerless, and insignificant?

> *Consider Aliya and Mazen. Aliya is known for being a good listener. Her friends and coworkers find it easy to share their concerns and challenges with her. She is easygoing and listens with her heart and empathetically. She is known for conveying warmth in her conversation. People feel heard and listened to. Mazen is not known as someone who listens. His tone is harsh and difficult. He is prone to gas lighting and manipulating. Coworkers and family members walk lightly around him as if they are walking on eggshells.*

Are Aliya and Mazen's communication styles complementary and compatible? Why? Why not? How do you imagine their styles impacting their relationship?

> *Consider Rasheeda and Dawud. Rasheeda grew up in a family that tends to yell, so she also tends to be loud and harsh in her communication. She is sarcastic and puts people down. She is not encouraging. She is impatient and is known for her lack of willingness to teach people what she knows. She is known as a difficult supervisor. She also actively gives to programs for the homeless in her community. Dawud's temperament is considered easygoing. He is known to listen objectively and to be a mediator in resolving problems and conflicts between friends and colleagues. He is known to be understanding and empathetic. He volunteers at a homeless shelter and food pantry.*

Are Rasheeda's and Dawud's communication styles complementary and compatible? Why? Why not? How do you imagine their styles impacting their relationship?

While they are both involved in community service that is not enough to sustain a relationship. Aggressive personality styles are not good for a long term healthy marriage.

Respect for one another is a critical aspect of communication. It is difficult to communicate with someone you don't respect. As Muslims you will want to keep Allah (swt) at the center of your relationship and your communication. Our conversations with each other should begin in the name of Allah with a brief dua in which you ask for mutual appreciation, understanding, discernment, and kindness. When we have Allah at the center of our relationship and our communication, we are reminded to be thoughtful and kind. We remember that we are brothers and sisters in humanity and in faith and that we don't want to harm each other physically or emotionally.

TAKE ACTION

How does this mouse make you feel?

Imagine you're in your living room while watching a movie. Suddenly out of nowhere a mouse is running around in the room. How do you feel? Not what do you think, but how do you feel? List your feelings here.

____

____

____

____

____

Now that you've listed how you feel, list why you feel the way you do. Where do your feelings about the mouse come from? Why do you feel the way you do about the mouse in your room?

____

____

____

____

____

Check in with friends or family nearby. Ask how they feel knowing that a mouse is running around the room.

So why is this important? This is important because it's all about how our experiences and messages about those experiences have impacted our perspective and our feelings. How do those experiences lead to what we believe in, feel, and how we communicate?

Another piece of the communication process is our ability to own our feelings and utilize the language of feelings, so that we can express how we truly feel. Often we use the few 'feelings' words we are used to, without realizing that the 'feelings' vocabulary is vast and allows us to expand and deepen our emotions. Happy, mad, glad, sad, and angry are just a few words in the feelings vocabulary but there are many more. Most of us don't have much experience expressing our feelings and many of us have a very limited feelings vocabulary. So rather than saying, "I feel disappointed when I haven't heard from you because I'm worried that something happened to you," one may pout or express anger. Sharing your feelings is a way of expressing them and taking ownership for them rather than blaming someone else.

TAKE ACTION

Feelings Vocabulary

Spend some time building your feelings vocabulary and practice using your feelings language in your various experiences at work, at school, and at home.

I-statements demonstrate recognition and ownership for our own feelings while clearly sharing our concern.

Fill in the phrase

"I feel ____________ when I ____________ because____________".

Use this as a kind of formula to capture your feelings, identify the situation, and own your feelings. This is not a blaming statement. Be careful not to blame the other person with statements like, "You make me feel angry when you come home late and don't call to let me know you're going to me late." Own your feelings and thoughtfully share them. A better way to say it could be, "I feel worried that something may have happened to you when I don't hear from you."

Reflective listening demonstrates sensitivity for others' experiences and feelings. It indicates that you are observant, empathetic, and caring which is good in healthy relationships. Below is an example of a reflective listening statement.

Ex: You seem worried about your grades because you were unable to complete your work on time.

You seem ____________ about____________ because ________.

See the appendix for the feelings vocabulary chart. I encourage you to start increasing your feelings vocabulary. Keep working your feelings vocabulary muscle because it will help you to express your feelings more clearly and openly.

It's important for us to own our feelings. It is important for us to recognize where our feelings come from as it relates to our own experiences and the messages and challenges and even the successes that we have had in life.

It is vital that you place yourself in an environment that facilitates good communication rather than presents obstacles to communication. It will be important to assess your communication style as it compares to your prospective spouse. A premarital counselor or coach will be helpful in determining whether your communication styles are compatible or have areas of conflict or disconnect. They can also help you develop and strengthen your communication skills with each other or help you determine that perhaps your styles are not compatible. Because communication is such an important aspect of a relationship, it will be important to have a communication style that is complementary and compatible. If not, then perhaps your prospect is not going to be a good fit and you may want to continue your matrimonial search.

Communication Style of the Prophet, (pbuh)

As we discussed earlier, the Prophet (pbuh) provides examples for us in life, marriage, our various relations, communication, and so much more. In the Seerah, there are examples of how he (pbuh) demonstrated good communication skills. He listened attentively to those who spoke in his presence. He, (pbuh), would turn his whole body toward the person that he was listening to, so he was not distracted and was able to clearly understand what they were conveying to him. He, (pbuh), wasn't looking at something or thinking about other things. He was focused on his conversation. He, (pbuh), was facing the person and listening to what they had to say. On one occasion a woman who experienced mental illness wanted to talk with the Prophet, (pbuh). He, (pbuh), let her know that he would talk with her and showed her respect that was uncommon for women to expect during that time. He did not stigmatize her because she had mental illness and even though she wasn't a leader or elite member of the community, he listened to her respectfully. He made her feel important and he demonstrated care and concern. And there was the blind man in Sura Abasa (80:8-10). The Prophet, (pbuh), was focused on the influential community leaders as he was trying to get them to come to Islam. In Sura Abasa, Allah revealed the importance of not neglecting or paying attention to the little people to impress the leaders. His example reminds us of the importance of giving your full attention no matter what the status of the person, demonstrating respect and empathy, and not being arrogant or neglectful of those with whom you are communicating. These behaviors are important in all our relationships, but most especially our spousal and family relationships.

Chapter 7

EXPECTATIONS AND COMPATIBILITY

Knowing what we expect and recognizing the importance of conveying our expectations before we get married is a key *Before the Nikah* principle. The ability to identify and express our expectations is critical, as we determine how compatible we are with our potential spouse. Most of us have expectations that we don't express. We don't talk about what we expect. We almost expect our significant other or spouse to guess or to know what we expect without having discussed it. Or we make assumptions that they are just like us. None of us are mind readers. The habit of not expressing our expectations or assuming that our spouse knows what we expect causes so much avoidable conflict. Everyone grew up differently, in a different family. Two siblings from the same family may have different expectations. For example, two siblings from the same large family have different expectations. One says, "I love large families and I want one too!" The other says large families are too much drama. If I have a family, I only want one child!" It is important that in the process of getting to know one another, we talk about what we expect, what we hope for, and what we want in our future marriage.

Areas we want to discuss in the process of getting to know each other include children, work, education, residence, money, health and wellness, and in-laws?

We want to talk about our expectations regarding children. Do we want our own biological children? Or do we want to adopt or foster? Some of us are not physically able to have our own biological children and some of us have decided that we can better help society by being an adoptive or foster parent. In any case, how many children do you want in your life? Whatever it is you want or expect, it is important to convey it to your prospective spouse.

Money is another big topic to cover. More will be discussed in a later chapter. It may not be covered in a first meeting, but certainly along the way you will want to discuss your views regarding money. How you handle money and your perspective of taking or paying interest will be important. Because of how we have been raised, we have different perspectives on money. Some of us have a strong focus on savings. Some of us don't save at all and don't care to save. Some of us are frugal. Others are miserly like Mr. Scrooge in the Charles Dickens classic. Our money mindset is related to how we were raised and how our families treated or viewed money. The Bible verse (1 Timothy 6:10), "For the love of money is the root of all evil," has impacted many people's mindset even though they are Muslim.

Others might see money in the hands of good people as the root of good deeds. Money is a way to give charity and support good causes. But in any case, whatever your views are, there needs to be a conversation about money. Financial concerns have caused many marital problems. How we spend money and how we save money, causes problems when we don't talk about it. Whether a couple should have one joint bank account for the household and then each have their own personal accounts is an issue for discussion. People have different ways of handling money. Also, be sure to discuss each other's perspective about a Muslim woman's money and property. Is there an expectation for the traditional view? Is the expectation that whatever she has or earns is hers to do with it as she pleases or is the view that she is expected to contribute to the household 50/50? Or is the expectation that no matter how much the wife makes, nothing of hers will be used for the family housing or standard of living. Will the husband's income be the only source, even if it puts the family's standard of living below what she is used to? Is there an understanding that even if he is the sole earner, the money is theirs not just his to give as he pleases? Will either parents' willingness to help with finances be accepted while the husband is in school or his career is getting started? It's important that you have a conversation before the nikah ceremony about what you expect and how money decisions will be made. Do not try to figure this out after you are married. If you can not discuss this matter before the marriage, who knows how it will be handled after the marriage.

Another area to discuss before marriage is work and education. Who will work? Who will go to school? These are all topics that are important to talk about prior to marriage.

Will both of you work outside the home? Will the wife work outside the home until she has children? Will she work part-time as the children come so she can keep her skills from her education or feel she is fulfilled? Will the husband have a business that gives him flexibility so he can work from home? Will the wife work outside the home, will they both be at home to trade-off caring for the children? Is she going to work while he raises the children? In today's gig economy, it is highly possible for both spouses must be able to work from home. As I write this book, we are in the middle of the coronavirus pandemic. Many couples are both working from home, if they still have their jobs. My husband and I are both working from home. Thank God we have the ability for both of us to do this. He has his office and I have mine. He has equipment from work here at the house and I have my own laptop that I'm working from. We don't have any young children, but we still have family responsibilities, and we really appreciate the flexibility, so that we can attend to some of those family responsibilities. For families with young children at this time during the coronavirus pandemic, school-age children are also at home and it's an adjustment for so many people. Whatever the case is, whether working from home is your preference or working outside the home, whether being an employee or an entrepreneur is your preference, it's a simple yet important conversation to have before you get married. It is an important conversation to have to avoid potential conflict or unexpressed expectations that lead to potential conflict.

Education is also important to discuss. What are your goals? If you don't have a successful business or investments, your educational decisions will impact how much you can afford once you get married? Do you have a scholarship or student loans that need to be repaid? Will you be responsible for your debt, or will your spouse or parents help to pay it? These are topics to discuss before you get married. Time and time again, I meet people who have conflicts about issues that could have been addressed and resolved before the nikah and during the courtship? They thought they had so much in common but there were these issues that seemed so small but turned out to be much bigger than they thought. An honest, open, transparent conversation may have prevented the conflict they are currently experiencing.

For many sex and intimacy is a challenging topic to discuss, but nonetheless, an important one. Many couples are having difficulty expressing needs and wants in this area. Many married couples are living more like roommates than loving spouses. Most couples have not had sex education before marriage. Pornography and infidelity are growing concerns. This is a topic that has to be discussed, but what do we discuss, when is the best time and how do we get to our important questions?

One way to get to the conversation may be to start with a question directed toward the parents and whether they demonstrated affection. Was your parents' relationship romantic when you were growing up? Did they share a bedroom? A bed? Were they comfortable with public displays of affection? Did you see them hug, hold hands, kiss? Do you consider yourself romantic? Did you know that the Prophet Muhammad, pbuh, was very romantic, loving, and patient in the way he treated his wives? Good communication skills and getting to know each other's love language are keys needed to have your conversations regarding sex and intimacy. Expectations are important to discuss. Someone married before must have known references. This is an important part of married life, so you want to make as informed a decision as possible. Attitudes around affection may really cause conflicts. One person may feel unloved or neglected or disrespected depending on how they demonstrate affection.

Where will you live? Will you live in a house or apartment, by yourselves or with your parents? Your residence and your in-laws are important topics to discuss. Are you going to be settled in one city or are you going to move around? I know for me as a child, I moved around a lot so I'm not much for moving around. I'm thankful my husband and I tended to be more settled. We have had the ability to be stable in terms of where we live. We made a big move across the country forty years ago; lived in the same city for all these years and the same home for the past twenty. However, not everyone likes to stay put. Some people are modern nomads and like to go where opportunity takes them.

Having a conversation about where you want to live and whether you want to move around for work or to explore different parts of the country and the world is one question you don't want to skip. Are you the kind of person who would prefer to be settled in one place is an important question. Do you see yourself living near your family or your prospective spouse's family or neither family? Do you see a place where you live close enough to the family that you can get to each other fairly quickly? Do you see yourself starting out in an apartment? Do you see continuing life in an apartment throughout your entire married life or working towards getting a house? If you get a house, how do you pay for it? Do you plan to take out a conventional mortgage or are you looking for an Islamic mortgage so that you are not paying "interest", or do you think it's better to rent? Are you going to live with in-laws or are in-laws going to live with you ? Do you see benefit in having your parents live with you so they can help with the kids, or will you live with your parents so you can save money or help your parents as they age? These are the kinds of questions that would be important to discuss before you get married.

In-law relationships in the immigrant Muslim community are often quite challenging and have placed a considerable strain on many marriages. Again, most couples did not have an open, honest discussion about their relationship with their in-laws before they married. A question about your perspective on in-laws can provide insight ? Do you see in-laws as your family? Are in-laws viewed as extended family support? Does your family see in-laws as taking their son or daughter away or are they giving you their daughter? It is important to get a sense of the relationship you're going to have with your in-laws and your parents. It is a must-know if you will be able to respect each other and your parents. It is also important to know if they are interfering in your relationship in a way that is not beneficial and how will you best handle it in a caring and respectful way.

I had to learn to be a mother-in-law and how to be supportive. It's something that you have to learn if you've never done it before. Both parties need to learn their boundaries. I'm very grateful that my daughter-in-law and I have good conversations about our common profession. She's smart and caring, a woman of faith, and she loves my son and my grandchildren. She calls me and I know I can call her directly. But not everybody has a relationship like that, and you don't always know what it's going to be like until you get into it. However, understanding what your expectations are about your relationships and clarifying boundaries before marriage is critical.

It is true you are marrying the family. Get to know in-laws and decide if you can work with the dynamic in their family and their family culture.

Discussing your perspectives about health and wellness are also important to explore before marriage. Knowing your values and beliefs about health, nutrition, and exercise before marriage lets you know if you are compatible and a good match. If you love to exercise and you're committed to exercise five times a week, and hiking and outdoor activities give you energy, while your prospective spouse is not interested in exercising but prefers watching television and doesn't get much exercise at all, are you a good fit? If you prefer a vegetarian, gluten-free diet and your spouse loves eating meat and potatoes or eating out, especially at fast food restaurants, will you be a good fit? Are there any health concerns such as diabetes, asthma, heart-related, or mental health issues? You would want to know! The lifestyle you prefer to live may impact your prospective spouse's health. You will want to make sure you have good health insurance coverage for ongoing care and treatment and that you are able to be sensitive and empathetic about your prospective spouse's health needs. You may have to learn how to support your spouse through an asthmatic episode, heavy cramping during her cycle, anxiety attacks, etc.

Meat, Music, Medhabs, Prayers and More

Our views on aspects of Islamic lifestyle have a lot to do with how we see ourselves in our practice of the religion. There are different views. Some mainstream, some less so. Aspects of Islamic tradition like halaal or zabiha meat, or whether you listen to music and what kind should all be part of your premarital conversations.

Whether or not you adhere to a particular madhab, school of thought, or adopt the idea that you don't need a specific one, should also be part of the Islamic life.

Questions to consider: What is your perspective about eating halal meat? Is halal the same as dhabiha where God's name is pronounced and stamped? Will you eat zabiha at home only? Not so strict? Is regular grocery store meat fine? Have you committed to eating meat from the halal meat market only? These are aspects of the life of a Muslim that are important to discuss. We eat everyday! You don't want conflict every single day! In addition to these areas, you may want to know how conscientious your prospective spouse is about praying the five daily prayers. Is praying fajr prayer important and on time before sunrise? Are you particular or not so particular about prayer? What does

Ramadan mean to you and what about attending and being involved in the mosque? What about friendships? Are your close friends practicing Muslims or not particularly religious of any faith? Are you comfortable with both of you spending time with friends from the opposite gender? Do you expect your prospective spouse to give up all friendships? These are questions about areas of life and the lifestyle you want to live that should be explored before marriage. Doing so enables you to determine whether or not you and a prospective spouse are a good fit for each other and allows you to make an informed decision rather than being in the dark about what to expect. **No need to force a relationship. Someone has the qualities or expectations that work for you and you have what will work for the right person for you. Don't force it!**

There is so much to consider before marriage, yet most people marry without discussing these important areas of life. We go into marriage expecting that we will have the same perspective, we will just work it out, or the other person will change to meet our way of thinking because of being in love. Share your thoughts and beliefs. Listen and give it time. Whether you agree with each other or have differing points of view, you will enter the marriage knowing what you are getting into with "informed consent."

TAKE ACTION

Expectations

Briefly write down your perspective on the above areas. Take time and give thought to your beliefs and expectations. (children, money, family, in-laws, health and wellness, sex and intimacy, meat, music, medhabs, prayer, education, residence). Use what you write here to help you share your expectations with your prospective spouse. Copy a blank ***Take Actions: Expectations*** sheet for your prospective spouse to also complete, so you can both share and exchange your thoughts.

Chapter 8

How Do You Get to Know Your Prospective Spouse?

Taking the time to truly get to know each other and determine if you are compatible is a core *Before the Nikah* principle.

How do you get to know your prospective spouse? How do you get to know if this person is a good fit for marriage and if you two are a good fit for marriage to each other? He may be a good fit for someone else but not for you. She may be just right for you. How do you know? How do you know the person you are discussing the possibility of marriage with is even who he says he is or who she says she is?

Getting to know your potential spouse takes so much more effort today because we live in a global society and so, many of us are not marrying the boy or girl next door. We aren't marrying someone we grew up with and played basketball, soccer, or jumped Double Dutch with. These aren't the people who you went to school with and spent time with them and their families. Today, so many are meeting and developing their relationships online. Most often, the people we are considering for marriage grew up hundreds and thousands of miles away in cities, towns, and villages quite different from our own. These are complete strangers, so getting to know each other requires a lot more effort than we needed to employ in the past.

By the time you meet, you will both have a lot of history that comes with you. You will have lots of messages that impact your beliefs, as well as a series of hurts, joys, and expectations that make up the person you have become.

So how will you truly get to "know" each other well enough to determine if you're ready for marriage and compatible for marriage with each other? To know someone means more than just seeing someone on Fridays at Jumu'ah prayers.

Knowing, according to Islam, means you have lived, traveled, or engaged in business together. If you haven't engaged in any or all of these activities, you don't know each other. You will then have to rely on those who honestly know your prospective spouse in these ways, to be honest with you about what they know of the person you are considering for marriage. Today references are hesitant to share what they know. Our desire to cover our brothers' faults takes precedence over our responsibility to be honest about what we know of a person being considered for marriage. This is not right. It is our duty to be honest. We will be held accountable for our part in conveying accurate information. This is why a professional non biased, third-party objective background check may be more helpful.

Islamic Tradition on how to truly know someone:

> *Kharashah ibnul Hurr (rahimahullah) reports that a man once testified in the presence of Caliph Umar(ra) who told him: 'I do not know you, and that is not an issue. Bring someone who does know you.' A man from the audience said: 'I know him.' Caliph Umar (ra) asked, 'What do you know about him?' The man replied: 'I know him*

to be reliable and virtuous.' At this, Caliph Umar (ra) asked him the following three questions: 1) Is he your close neighbor, who day and night are known to you? 2)Did you deal with him with monetary affairs, which could give you an idea of his piety? 3) Was he ever your companion on a journey, from which you could have seen his character? The man replied in the negative to each of these questions. Umar (ra) said to him: 'You do not know him.' He turned to the witness and said: 'Bring someone who knows you.' (Sunanul Kubra of Bayhaqi, vol. 10 p 125)

Remember you're not ready for marriage if you haven't taken time to get to know about the person you are considering from those who know them. Time is key for people to really reveal their true selves.

Many of our community members, even religious leaders, believe that having observed someone pray at the masjid is sufficient to know a person. Remember the various ways Khadijah (ra) observed young Muhammad (pbuh) before she proposed marriage.

Consider young Waheedah's experience. Rashad and his family lived in her hometown when she was young. Then he and his family moved away during Rashad's junior high and high school years. They then moved back when he was in his early twenties to operate the family business. After they had been back for some time and the business was up and running, Rashad's parents asked Waheedah's parents if they could discuss their children marrying, since Rashad was interested in Waheedah. Waheedah and her family gave the proposal serious consideration, and as part of their exploring the possibility, Waheedah spoke with the imam of the local mosque and asked what he knew of Rashad. The imam told her that he prayed at the mosque regularly and that this was all she needed to know to know that he would make a good and compatible spouse. She and her family took the information from the imam into serious consideration, along with what they observed and decided to accept the proposal.

It turns out their marriage was a disaster. Rashad turned out to be abusive and difficult at home, and their marriage was short lived. While they were apart, it turns out he had a string of relationships that were abusive, and no one told her before they got married.

There are many aspects to a person. We know from Sura Al-Baqara (2:1-20) and Sura Al-Ma'un (107) among other verses in the Qur'an and stories in the Seerah, that there are many people who show different sides of themselves at home and in public. We know that there are those who pray just to be seen rather than with sincerity, so beware of making this your sole criteria for knowing a person's character.

So what do you need to know about your marriage prospects and how will you learn about each other? This should not be one sided. Both sides should be getting to know each other. If she is doing all the inquiry, and he isn't trying to get to know about her, this is one-sided and may be a warning sign. Conversely, if he is trying to get to know her, but she isn't asking about him, this is cause for concern. To get to know each other takes time and interest in the various aspects of each other's life.

In addition to the prospective spouse's name and age, which you will want to verify before signing the marriage documents, you will want to know about the same things you asked yourself when you completed your personal self assessment. You will also want to know about each other's personality and temperament, relationship with Islam, practice of Islam, connection with the Muslim community, social skills, educational level, work history, marital/relationship history, communication style, socioeconomic status, values, and expectations for you and your marriage. You will want to know if your intended spouse is still resolving a past relationship or in the midst of a dissolution emotionally and legally? You will want to know about each other's physical, mental, and emotional health. Are there any chronic or acute mental or physical problems that you are experiencing? How do you both address health and wellness? Do either of you have children? What is your custody arrangement and parental visitation plan? Do you have past or pending legal or financial matters that may impact your relationship going forward?

You will want to know about each other's family and your relationship with them. What is your family's expectation for your marriage?

Why do you want to marry? Why do you want to marry each other? What is your intention?

Getting to know someone for marriage takes time.

Time is temporal and experiential. It involves hours and months and seasons as well as life experiences. You are encouraged to get know your prospective spouse over time as it relates to the points that Umar (ra) outlined for the man who was to be a witness as well the time young Muhammad (pbuh) was observed in working for Khadijah (ra) before she proposed. We find Muslims being encouraged to hurry to marriage to prevent the risk of premarital sexual activity rather than encouraging the prospective couple to take this time seriously and use the time to get to know about each other. This is a recipe for disaster and is ripe for abuse. I cringe when I hear people met and got married in the pandemic. This time was not normal. Many states had placed residents on stay at home orders. Many of us did not visit friends or close relatives for more than a year for many of us. It is important to get to know the person when the world opens and is no longer on lock down. Will you both still be able to relate. Will you love to go out or prefer to stay in?

The period between meeting one another and signing the nikah contract should be used to assess each other's character, veracity, religiosity, empathy, humility, and potential for compassion/rahma, love/muwada and tranquility/sakinah.

It is important for your families to talk with each other. You are marrying each other and each other's family. Your family and friends should talk with both of you. Your Marriage Success Team, parents, wali conduct a background check to verify identity, legal history, and relationship with the Muslim community. You may even seek the expert assistance of a private investigator. The purpose of using an expert is not for unethical intentions but rather to corroborate the information that has been shared and to obtain the information that may not have been provided.

How will you get to know this information about each other?

The period between meeting and engagement with the intention to marry is referred to as courtship. It may also be called dating with the intention to marry. The courtship period can vary. This period will be used to determine if the prospective couple will go on to engagement and marriage. This is the stage in which the couple will want to take time to get to know each other's expectations, values, dreams, and discuss other topics mentioned in earlier chapters, if they have not already gathered that information. Traditionally practicing Muslims are mindful of not being alone and placing themselves in a position which might lead to sex before marriage.

Spending time with friends and family, attending events, conferences, meeting in public cafes, hanging out in the living room while the family is moving about the rest of the house, and going on outdoor chaperoned activities are ways to spend time and get to know each other. This period has to be purposeful to accomplish the goal and have the important questions answered. Many are also meeting through online matrimonial sites or online communities and then taking their interest offline to meet in person and to connect with family and friends.

How will you get to know each other? Certainly, you will talk with each other, ask questions, and listen to each other's answers. *Soul Search,* a set of cards available through **TherapywithAya.com**, enables prospective couples to learn about each other through cards that help you ask purposeful questions. Imam Magid's Premarital Questionnaire and Munira Ezzeldine *Before the Wedding,* also provide questions you will want to address prior to marriage. You want to listen to the answers with purpose. People spend years dating and hanging out and never get to the important or hard questions. Be careful to listen and not engage in confirmation bias.

The Before the Nikah Vetting Process

I have shared a variety of questions and resources for what you will want to learn about each other. In this section, I have included the proprietary *Before the Nikah Vetting Process* as a step-by-step way to investigate your prospective spouse's background and corroborate the information you have learned.

The Vetting Process

Goal: To have informed consent and gauge compatibility of a person for a life-long partnership in light of this global era. To have a system you can implement and enlist others to assist you. To reduce the risk of marrying someone incompatible (also known as Tie your camel).

Focus your courting so that you can accomplish all of the following steps.

Run each viable prospect through each step of this system. Having the system prevents confirmation bias which leads to confirmation blindness. Remember, getting a job has an interview, vetting process, and probationary period. Deciding on a marriage partner deserves the same care.

Have the written list handy of your absolutes, what you can hold with, and what are your deal breakers. Be honest about your motive for wanting to be married (partnership, not to be lonely, hormones, feeling old, have a caretaker? Have a sugar daddy/sugar mama? To rebel against your parents' rigidity? Get out of the house?)

Enlist your Marriage Support Team (MST). Share your list with them and see that they support your perspective and vision for your future spouse (*shura*). Who is on your MST? (List their names and invite them together)

It's ok to discuss timeframes. But, don't set a wedding date before completing each step. Having a wedding date promotes confirmation bias which can lead to confirmation blindness.

Be a whole self, not half of a person who needs to be completed. Have a healthy sense of self-esteem, self-worth, and self-confidence when engaging in this process. All of your senses should be awake when engaging in this process. If you're feeling "too down, too sad, depressed, lonely, feeling poor, feeling fat, feeling ignorant, feeling broken or feeling unworthy," heal yourself BEFORE entering this process. Get therapy, bibliotherapy, educate yourself, so that you can heal. Otherwise you can be too befogged and miss key information. That kind of vulnerable state can cloud your judgment. Also, manipulative people smell vulnerability like a wolf and will seek to exploit you.

Now Begin

(Go through each step. Don't miss a step. Give yourself time.
Remember marriage is not just for this life, it's for the next too)

- ❏ Ask questions related to what a life would be like with this person (like 100 questions by Imam Magid in the back of *Before you Tie the Knot,* play ice-breaker card games, and answer your self-assessment questions. Ask them what you asked yourself. Ask similar questions in different ways. Listen to their answers. Then corroborate their answers through their actions and background checking. If they tell you one thing, but their actions are another thing, that is a red flag. Leave no stone unturned. Understand the motive of why this person wants to marry you. This is where time comes in. Don't rush. Observe them through *the seasons.*

- ❏ Believe nothing, verify everything. Don't create a narrative about this person. Find out who they really are. Ask and confirm.

- ❏ Interact with the prospective partner (without sex, not alone, semiprivate).

- ❏ Ensure that your wali and MST have regular interaction with your prospective spouse and ask questions to gauge compatibility. Make sure your Wali and MST know you, what's on your list, and have bought into your list so they are on board with you. This is also so they know what to vet for. You want to get their honest assessment over time.

- ❏ Ensure your closest circle interacts with prospective spouse, such as your friends, work colleagues, etc. These are the important people in your world who also know you and what to vet for.

- ❏ Conduct a discreet background check (find out who you know knows this person and seek their anonymous opinion). If no one knows this person, stay away. *You may not have a tribe, but someone has to know your reputation.*

- ❏ Conduct a formal background check.

- ❏ Learn/experience their world (not a visit, not a vacation, not with your last dollar). These are the places where they spend the bulk of their time and history to the point where you know them in their natural environment, where you know the pros and cons of their cultural variations, cultural differences and cultural expectations, and their true personality.

- ❏ See if your prospective spouse takes the time to learn/experience your world to the point where it is not just a visit, not a vacation, and not with his/her last dollar. They come to know the places where you spend the bulk of your time and history to the point where they know you in your natural environment, where they know the pros and cons of your cultural variations, cultural differences and cultural expectations, and your true personality. If they are not taking the time and investment to know you, stay away.

- ❑ Within a year of meeting each other, each of you take Dr. Nadir's *Before the Nikah Marriage Preparation Course*™ (for a minimum of 12 weeks) separately or together (together allows you to hear the same things and converse).
- ❑ Make dua throughout, rely on Allah (pray Salatul Istikhara and make other informal prayers for guidance and discernment).
- ❑ Hire a counselor for premarital or individual counseling when there are issues you want to work on (like blending a family, in-law challenges, cross-cultural challenges, past traumas, etc.)
- ❑ Trust your gut/listen to your intuition (These are signs of Allah).
- ❑ Don't fill in the blanks or your own story.
- ❑ Hire an attorney to understand the legal implications this marriage will have on you financially and personally. (Consider a prenuptial agreement, marriage in your state versus another, international marriage, etc.)

Remember:

1. If it feels wrong, it is wrong.
2. If she/he is trying too hard, if it looks like their effort involves too much conspicuous and ostentatious effort, it is fake.
3. If it seems too good to be true, it probably is.
4. Believe nothing, verify everything. Ninety percent of the time people lie (even good people put on their best face/the mask).

The proper adab for the vetting process - exercise confidentiality, discretion, honesty, make the intention to assess compatibility for marriage (not to expose, shame, blackmail, or get juicy gossip).

Next Steps:

After you are confident you know them, they know you, and this relationship is a good fit for your dunya and will help get you to Jannah, confirm a wedding date. Discuss mahr, marriage contract terms, prenuptial agreements, etc.

The Marriage Support Team or MST

It takes a "village to raise a child" and a trusted and knowledgeable support system to assist you in choosing wisely and vetting your prospective spouse. That Marriage Support Team or MST is comprised of trusted members of your support system who have come together to provide you with wise counsel in the process of your search for your future spouse. Your MST also helps you vet the matrimonial prospects on the way to determine the one that is the best fit for you.

Your MST may include your parents, your wali, your siblings, your best friend, your aunt or uncle or others who know, value, and love you They are people whose opinions you value and respect. If you are a convert to Islam don't hesitate to include your family of other faith traditions, as long as they support your commitment to Islam and live the life of a practicing Muslim. Your MST is dedicated to what is best to help you meet the person who is compatible and the best fit for you to have a healthy long lasting marriage. These people know you. They are in agreement with you about what is best for you. They know what you want in a future spouse. They are dedicated to asking the hard questions and being honest with you about whether you and your matrimonial prospect will be good for each other. They sincerely care about you. Members of your MST know your values, they know what you are looking for in a prospective spouse, they are in agreement with your views and what would make a healthy relationship for you. They understand the courtship, vetting, and marriage process similarly to the way you understand it. They are committed to being open, honest, and sincere with you about their concerns and what they see. They will not paint a rose colored picture when they believe you are not a good fit for each other. They will give you their honest, sincere, objective view of marriage with your intended spouse. To work with your MST, you should feel comfortable listening to their views and having them help you vet your prospect. Some of the members of your MST will converse with your matrimonial prospect. Others will be observers and other members will assist with making sure the background checking is complete. It is important to know that the matrimonial selection process is an important aspect in a future healthy marriage. It takes time. It takes a village or in this case your Marriage Support Team. InshaAllah your MST will be with you throughout your courtship, engagement, wedding, as well as the ups and downs, the successes, and challenges of your marriage in hopes of helping you and your future spouse to a loving, compassionate, sakinah-filled long lasting union. They believe in helping you build a healthy marriage that will help you both get to heaven. While this may not sound like a Hollywood Romance which is neither practical nor realistic, inshaAllah this will be a sincere effort to help you choose wisely, determine if you're a good fit for each other, and help you prepare for a healthy, loving married life.

I take no pleasure in pointing out that there are people who intentionally lie. However, many of us in our kindness, ignorance, and naiveté welcome people into the intimate spaces of our lives without a thorough understanding of who they are and whether or not what they are telling us is true and honest. Remember that truly knowing someone means knowing who they are in their morning and nighttime living space, knowing how they handle money and business transactions, and what they are like when traveling with them.

Nothing can account for downright liars, swindlers, con artists, or green card scammers. You have to do your best background check with the help of your Marriage Support/Success Team. Don't skip steps in the proprietary *Before the Nikah* Vetting Process. I know this is not very romantic, however informed consent is your right. You have a right to make your decision with all the cards on the table.

Stop!

You've got to know when to hold 'em. Know when to fold em,
Know when to walk away and know when to run!

from The Gambler
Song by Kenny Rogers

TAKE ACTION

Profile of Your Prospective Spouse

Take the time to compile the profile you imagine for your prospective spouse. Begin the process here. What are you looking for in your potential mate?

Chapter 9

Zero Tolerance for Domestic Violence

Zero tolerance for domestic violence is a key *Before the Nikah* principle.

Islam prohibits any type of oppression and does not support or justify family violence, abuse, or oppression against women or children. Domestic violence is a form of oppression. According to Alwani and Abugideri (2003), oppression occurs when mercy and justice are ignored. They further state that Islam defines oppression as transgressing limits or boundaries defined by God. It prohibits oppression at all levels of society from the basic spousal unit to the family, the community, nationwide society, and global society. Islam promotes justice and healthy relationships as we see in many verses of the Qur'an and the example of the family life and traditions of Prophet Muhammad (pbuh). Allah tells us in the Qur'an to stand firmly for justice.

While there are those who justify domestic oppression using verses of Qur'an, they are taking verses and meanings out of context to suit their own ends in contradiction to the message of Islam. As a community, we have been in a state of denial regarding the existence of domestic violence among Muslims in the U.S. We have been naive and found it hard to believe in light of the stereotypes and Islamophobia our community has been fighting.

However, the horrific murder and beheading of Aasiya Zubair, the founder of Bridges TV, by her husband in 2009 "sent a shockwave through our collective consciousness," according to Project Sakinah. It lifted the veil that had been over our eyes. If we didn't believe domestic violence existed in the American Muslim community before we could no longer deny it.

Domestic violence is real. The anecdotal evidence and the growing research let us know that Muslims like Christians, Jews, and other faith and non-faith traditions experience this public health crisis. According to the Center for Disease Control, one in four women and one in ten men will experience intimate partner violence at some point in their lifetimes. Statistics indicate that every 18 seconds someone is a victim of domestic violence. Domestic violence occurs without regard to religion, race, age, gender or sexual orientation, or socioeconomic status.

"A survey of 801 American Muslims found that 31% reported experiencing abuse within an intimate partner relationship and 53% reported experiencing some form of domestic violence during their lifetime." (Peaceful Families & Project Sakinah 2011 DV Survey)

Domestic violence shows up in various forms including physical, emotional, sexual, economic, psychological, and religious abuse. In a survey of nine domestic violence organizations around the U.S. serving nearly 2,000 Muslim women survivors, executive directors reported that survivors experienced various forms of abuse including 82% emotional or verbal abuse, 65% financial abuse, 49% spiritual abuse, 74% physical abuse, and 30% sexual abuse. (Alkhateeb 2010)

During your matrimonial search it is important to be awake and aware. It is important to step into your search with recognition that there are people in the pool of prospects who are not kind, loving, and empathetic. While there are certainly kind, loving, compassionate people in the pool, there are also people who are oppressive, unkind, hurtful, manipulative, and narcissistic. Most of us don't want to believe it, but we have to take the blinders off and choose wisely.

What can you do to prevent going into an abusive, oppressive marriage?

1. Be aware of the warning signs or red flags of intimate partner violence.
2. Learn and practice skills that promote positive, compassionate, loving relationships (positive communication skills, positive coping skills, conflict resolution skills, mutual consultation, and problem solving skills)
3. Develop your iman. Develop internal God consciousness (taqwa) within.
4. Learn to recognize the green flags and put the positive behavior into practice.
5. Implement the steps in the *Before the Nikah* Vetting Process.
6. Utilize your Marriage Support Team to vet prospects for potentially abusive behavior.
7. Participate in a marriage preparation course.
8. Participate in premarital counseling to assess readiness.
9. Choose wisely!

It is important to study the red flag warning signs so that you are able to recognize them in your prospective spouse. Red flag means STOP! Seeing a pattern of any of these signs is a warning to NOT continue with the relationship.

What are the red flags or warning signs that may indicate that someone is abusive?

Below are some of the warning signs you will want to look out for before marriage, during courtship:

- *Manipulates the truth*

- *Insincere*
- *Evasive*
- *Arrogant-never wrong*
- *Self-centered-lack appreciation for other's perspective*
- *Ethnocentric*
- *Holds a grudge*
- *Lacks empathy*
- *Possessive or jealous behavior*
- *Controlling behavior*
- *Using force to resolve problems*
- *Severe mood swings*
- *Expressing rigid ideas about gender roles*
- *Minimizing abusive behavior*
- *Gaslighting (manipulates someone psychologically to question their own sanity)*
- *Not wanting you to consult your Marriage Support Team*
- *Keeping you up all night even though you have work or school the next day*
- *Love Bombing*

Additional Red flag warning signs you may see during marriage:

- *Taking your money or refusing to give you money for your expenses*
- *Preventing you from working, going to school, or participating in hobbies/activities you enjoy*
- *Preventing/keeping you from seeing friends or family*
- *Constantly criticizing and demeaning your parental skills*
- *Threatening to take away your children*

(Sources:peacefulfamilies.org/faq.html;Archie Aquino, LPC)

Below are some of the green flags you want to see to let you know you can continue forward cautiously. Look for a consistent pattern of behavior around this behavior. Once is not enough. You want to see signs over a span of time in various experiences before you commit to marriage.

Some Green Flags:

- Taqwa-God consciousness
- Trust
- Honesty
- Authenticity
- Consistency and integrity
- Clear and safe communication
- Accountability
- Humility
- Self-awareness and personal insight
- Maturity
- Forgiveness
- Empathy
- Appreciation of diverse cultures and traditions
- Encouragement
- Supportive
- Sincere concern for your health and wellness

Consider the story of Sister Halima.

Sister Halima is a mature sister who arrived in her new city having left her business and family to start her new life with her soon-to-be husband. When she arrived, she was happy and looking forward to marriage and living in her new home. Sister Halima was a smart, stately, self-assured woman when she arrived. She had owned her own business and was well-connected at home. However, by the time she was able to get out of the marriage she had such hope for, she was emotionally broken and her teeth had been knocked out from domestic abuse. She was devastated financially, emotionally, and spiritually.

The thing is, he was known for abusing women, but no one told her. She didn't find out the person he was until after she married him. She might have decided that they were not a good fit for each other but she wasn't given the opportunity to make that choice. She was not able to make an INFORMED decision. He wasn't honest and neither were the people who introduced them fully open and honest about the kind of person he was.

What might have been some red flags for our sister?
What could have been done to prevent the devastating outcome?

The Era of Narcissism

The past five years have been referred to as the era of narcissism by Dr. Ramani Durvsula, a well-known licensed clinical psychologist and expert on the subject. During this time we have witnessed a consistent rise in narcissism and narcissistic behavior. Most of us didn't know what it was and even though we had seen some of the behaviors, we didn't know what to call it. Because this behavior is becoming more prevalent and is another level of abuse, it is important to be aware of how narcissistic behavior reveals itself. It is also important to look out for it in your matrimonial search process and to give yourself adequate time and a variety of situations in which to observe your prospective spouse.

Dr Ramani defines narcissism as a consistently toxic pattern characterized by entitlement, grandiosity, lack of empathy, validation seeking, superficiality, interpersonal antagonism, insecurity, hypersensitivity, contempt, arrogance, and poor emotional regulation (especially rage). Narcissism is an interpersonally toxic pattern.

Consider the story of Tariq and Zoraida. Tariq called Zoraida one day, seemingly out of nowhere, via Whatsapp. Since she didn't know him, she ignored the call. He didn't speak English and she didn't speak Arabic, so she continued to ignore the call. But Tariq was persistent and even got a friend to translate for him and convinced Zoraida to speak with him. He was charming and humorous and up on current events in the U.S. He told Zoraida that a mutual friend recommended her to him and suggested that they would be right for each other. She was hesitant but continued to talk to him as he learned English. He asked her not to take him for granted. He seemed kind and caring and able and ready to enjoy marriage to a successful professional woman. In their conversations, she explored his interest in moving to the U.S. since she was not willing to leave her career and move to his home country. He seemed to be the real deal; loving, attentive, easygoing, family-oriented, attractive, and practicing Islam in a balanced way. So within four months, after asking all the questions and getting all the right answers, Zoraida flew to Egypt with her Aunt Sarah to meet his family. While she was there, they did the nikah ceremony with her father and mother over zoom.

The day after the nikah, the mask began to peel off. He revealed he was in a car accident and sustained a head injury. He also said he was in the middle of a lawsuit and got frequent headaches. He became controlling and would not respect her work and sleep schedule. His angry temper, lack of empathy, and gaslighting began to reveal itself. Zoraida questioned the relationship but believed him when he said he was sorry. And she hoped for the days of the loving Tariq to return. He assured her that he was just stressed but once he moved to the U.S. and they got settled, everything would be just fine. He arrived. They married in 90 days under U.S. law in a nice wedding with a few of their friends and family. They submitted the paperwork for his green card. When he received his green card, he flipped and started distancing himself. It became clear that Tariq had love bombed Zoraida to obtain his green card, so he could settle in the U.S. Zoraida didn't realize how someone who was so loving over the past four months could change so profoundly.

This story reveals the existence of narcissistic behavior which Zoraida had not been familiar with. She had heard presentations about the cycle of domestic violence but she had never learned about narcissism. The importance of giving behaviors time observing behavior in a person over seasons, conducting a thorough background check, and not engaging in confirmation bias became apparent as lessons from this story.

How to recognize red flags and narcissistic behaviors are lessons you want to learn without going through this experience personally. Zoraida also learned that some seemingly religious people are dishonest and use the immigration system to meet their needs. Certainly this is not the case for everyone. That is why you want to pray istikhara prayer and do your due diligence, trust your intuition, and rely on Allah to guide you to what is best. It is also important to give the relationship time and work with your marriage support team to take your prospect through the vetting process.

TAKE ACTION

1. Attend *Peaceful Families Project* seminars to learn more about domestic abuse.

2. Explore Dr Ramani's Youtube videos to learn more about narcissism and how to recognize it.

3. Participate in the *Before the Nikah* Institute's Marriage Preparation course.

4. Become part of the *Before the Nikah* community to gain support from other community members who have taken or are taking the course.

Chapter 10

Money Mindset, the Mahr and the Law

Your compatibility regarding money, how you save it, how you spend it, and the place it has in your life will have a significant impact on your marriage. Conflict about finances and money matters are listed among the top issues that negatively impact marital health and can lead to the breakdown of the relationship. **Discussing money matters and money mindset before the marriage are a key *Before the Nikah* principle.**

Money views

Your discussion should include your money mindset, how you view money, and financial values. It is critical to be self-aware and know the important questions to ask. Some questions to ask include: What are your financial values? Did you grow up in a wealthy family? Was your family of modest means? How did your parent's way of handling money and your family's financial circumstance affect your view of money? Are you someone who would only buy used cars? Or are you of the mindset that it is safer for your family to own and drive new cars? What is your credit score? What is your perspective on credit cards and interest-bearing accounts and savings? Are you frugal? Are you generous with your family? Are you miserly? Do you pay your zakat and additional sadaqa as much as possible? What is your view of residual income, stocks, and real estate income? What is your perspective of insurance? Larry Smith, businessman, says one of his life lessons is, "if there are different financial values between two people, especially spouses, there are automatic problems in the relationship." It is better to have this discussion before marriage so that you can decide if your perspective is compatible regarding one of the most challenging issues couples experience.

The Mahr

The mahr is a requirement for marriage. Some translate mahr as a marriage gift. For a marriage to be official according to Islam, the groom is required to provide it. Some call it a dowry. It is really an obligation to demonstrate sincerity as a husband and his care for his wife. It is also a way of demonstrating his intention to provide financial support for her. It is not a bride-price. It is not an amount to be given to or by the parents for taking their daughter. It is not a gift that can be given or not. It is not optional. It is not based on her worth as a woman, her virginity, or previous marital status. While she may choose to waive it, he still has to be prepared to offer her the mahr. It is prescribed in the Qur'an and the traditions of Prophet Muhammad (pbuh). According to Lisa Hashem, of Muslim Women and Finance, the mahr is likely the first financial transaction you and your spouse will engage in. This can be a test of how your money discussions will go in marriage.

The challenge regarding the Mahr is that most do not know its purpose or how much it should be, or when it should be given. It is usually handled very privately, so people outside of the immediate family don't know much about it. During the time of the Prophet Muhammad, (pbuh), he said no limit could be placed on the mahr. During the caliphate of Umar (ra) when he attempted to limit the mahr, a woman stood up to challenge him which forced him to reaffirm what the Prophet (pbuh) had said, that no limit could be placed on the mahr. The mahr is negotiated between the prospective bride and groom. While the bride and groom can get assistance from their family or wali to negotiate, the bride and groom have the final say. The mahr is determined based upon his means, his resources, and what she wants. He can get help to provide the mahr. For example, according to Shaykh Mendes in his course, *Black Lives Around the Messenger*, on the marriage of the Prophet (pbuh) to Umm Habiba Ramla, the daughter of Abu Sufyan, the Negus of Abysinnia gave her a mahr of 400 dinars approximately $101,232 on the Prophet Muhammad's behalf. Also Khadijah (ra) used to sponsor the mahr for men of her community. In some cultures it is customary to get help from family or close neighbors. If the prospective bride's standard of living is beyond his means or out of his league, this may be a sign that they will not be compatible and they may be better suited for someone from a similar socio economic background.

The thing that is most concerning and why this has been included here is because real talk rarely occurs about the mahr. Too often, the mahr is delayed, so then it becomes obligatory to be given on divorce or death. However, approximately 99% of the time in America, women do not get their mahr because the brothers renege on their agreement and there are no Islamic courts or community pressure to ensure it is enforced. The mahr agreement is rarely enforced in U.S. civil courts. Given the reality of Muslim life in the U.S. I teach that the mahr should be a demonstration of the prospective groom's sincerity as a husband, his ability to care for his future wife, his financial means, and a reflection of the way she was accustomed to being cared for. It should be given at the time of the marriage ceremony rather than delayed because in the U.S. if it is not given at the ceremony, she almost never gets it. He should obtain help from other sources to give the mahr and not ask his future wife to carry the debt of his mahr.

One recommendation is that boys grow up establishing a mahr fund just like they have a car fund, a college fund, or a business development fund. Muslim boys should grow into Muslim men who plan for marriage, expect to marry, and prepare to take on their responsibilities, starting with providing their future wife with her mahr. Parents should start a mahr fund for their son just like they start a college fund. I have two Muslim sons, and I did not realize how important this would be when they became adults and were ready for marriage. I did not know anything about this, but now that I know, I would recommend my grandsons and nephews have a mahr fund started for them, and they continue it when they start earning income.

The mahr is connected in so many ways to how a future bride and groom view each other. The prospective bride wants to know that her future husband will love, honor, and take care of her. She wants to feel secure in knowing that she is being taken care of, even if she has the financial means to take care of herself. The prospective husband should see himself as responsible for his family and respectful of his wife demonstrating care and concern for her.

The mahr should be of value. It does not have to be but often it is cash money, gold bars, gold jewelry, income producing real estate, or a home that appreciates in value with the deed in her name. Ideally it is an amount she could use to start a new life or care for herself if need be. It is hers alone to do what she wants with it. It is not an emergency fund to pay household bills, a savings fund for the children's college, a vacation fund, or for her to buy things her husband is responsible for.

The mahr should encourage both parties to be more discerning about who would be a compatible lifelong partner who would help them get to Jannah. Just as much as one would take their time exploring their possible new home, a prospective spouse should take time and effort to see if they are a good fit for their possible spouse. Aya Rasheed, Marriage and Family Therapist and Dahir Nasser, Diversity and Inclusion Consultant, recommend thinking of the time and input one would put into marriage as an even greater investment than the time and effort one would put into choosing their new home. In choosing a new home one would hire a housing inspector, research the background on the house, speak with the neighbors, check with the Chamber of Commerce, check out the local social media about the area, and the schools in the area. One's choice of spouse is about who will help you get to Heaven, who will be the parent of your children, who will help you care for your parents in their old age, and who will work with you to fulfill your career goals. One should give the selection of a future spouse more consideration than the next home. The choice of your future spouse is one of the most important considerations of your life. Brothers, you took time and focus to raise the mahr. You will want it to be a reflection and demonstration of your commitment. Sisters the mahr is a demonstration of his commitment. You want to explore his intentions, sincerity, veracity, and you do not want him to be in debt to you for this obligation and risk not fulfilling his commitment. Most often people do not even talk about the mahr or what the consequences or realities of delaying the mahr might be. In this society, for the most part, if the groom does not give the mahr by the signing of the nikah or marriage agreement, the bride likely will not be able to collect it in the future. And unfortunately the groom will carry this spiritual debt on his shoulders until the Day of Judgment. Nobody wants that.

The legal side of marriage

Recognizing the legal aspects of marriage, discussing, and preparing for them before marriage are key *Before the Nikah* principles.

There are a variety of legal matters that activate upon marriage, but most of us are not aware of what they are. The law is all around us and part of our lives. If we are unaware of the marriage related laws, we can become victims of it. As Muslims, not only are you getting married according to Islamic law, but you are also getting married according to the law of the land. There are no Islamic courts in the U.S. to address

Islamic family law. The *Before the Nikah* course will help you identify legal matters in order to prepare individuals for selecting their future spouse, as well as for couples in various phases of their married life. Attorney Zarinah Nadir, author of *Legally Savvy*, recommends consulting with an attorney, and utilizing the prenuptial agreement as a tool to legally document your agreement prior to getting married. Failure to consult an attorney prior to marriage may lead you to be surprised that the agreements you made as a couple are not upheld or enforced within the civil legal context.

It is important to know if you live in a community property or separate property state. Most of us don't have any idea what type of state we live in and it may impact us upon marriage or upon dissolution of marriage. Family law is state specific. We also don't know how congruent or not Islamic law is with the U. S. law. What will be your rights and responsibilities if you opt for a religious contract only and how will you enforce those rights? What if you decide to obtain a state marriage license and get married Islamically? If you don't marry with a state license in most U.S. states, you are not married according to U.S. law. Most states do not recognize common law marriage. Attorney Zarinah Nadir reminds us that the lack of a state issued marriage license can affect your federal entitlements, taxes, social security benefits, and possible pension. Without a license, you are not entitled to the rights of a married couple, such as making medical decisions, funeral arrangements, visitation in the hospital intensive care unit, and other rights that would usually be entitled to a spouse.

If you are married religiously as a second, third, or fourth wife, you are not entitled to a civil state marriage license in the U. S. since polygynous marriage is against U. S. law. Without a state issued marriage license, you are not entitled to Federal benefits. A woman who is married in polygny and whose husband has not named them as a beneficiary in a will or other legal document will likely have no claim to assets. Remember the story of Asma who married into a polygynous marriage without knowing what she was getting into?

TAKE ACTION

Before you marry, speak with an attorney and your prospective spouse about the answers to these questions.

These and other questions should be discussed before the marriage ceremony so you can make an informed decision.

Is your prospective spouse religiously married?   Yes   No

If yes, and the prospective spouse is the man, how many "wives" does he have?

Is your prospective spouse legally married?   Yes   No

Has he or she been married before?

If so, is it over officially and legally? And emotionally?

Does your prospective spouse have children from a previous relationship(s)?

If so, is custody, sole, joint/shared?

Is the state (or province) you plan to marry in a community or separate property state?

How are religious only, non civil license marriages viewed by state law?

In your social circles? In your mosque community?

What federal benefits are spouses with a state license entitled to?

What are the prospective spouses' perspectives regarding separate and community property? Is it aligned with your understanding of Islamic law?

What are the benefits of writing and signing the Islamic marriage contract?

What are the benefits and drawbacks of a legally prepared prenuptial agreement?

What are the benefits and drawbacks of a legally prepared Last Will and Testament, Powers of Attorney and Medical Directive for religiously married people? For those married with a state license?

____

____

____

____

____

____

____

____

____

Qur'an

And among His signs is that He created you from dust, then-behold!-you are human beings spreading over the earth. Rum 30:20

And among His signs is that He created for you spouses from among yourselves so that you may find comfort in them and He has placed between you compassion and mercy. Surely in this are signs for people who reflect. Rum 30:21

And among His signs is the creation of the heavens and the earth, and the diversity of your languages and colors, Surely in this are signs for those of sound knowledge. Rum 30:22

We created you in nations and tribes that you may know one another. Hujurat 49:13

Chapter 11

Cross Cultural Marriage and In-Laws

Clarity regarding individual and family views on cross-cultural marriage and interfaith marriage before you marry is a key *Before the Nikah* principle.

Humanity is blessed to have been created in diverse races, languages, and perspectives as we observe in life and see in various verses of the Qur'an, traditions of Prophet Muhammad, and summarized in his (pbuh) last sermon. Be honest with yourself about the role of diversity in your future marriage. What does your family say on this? What are your parents' views and wishes?

Allah created humanity. He made us all so different. We are different in our skin tones, languages, hair textures, our likes and dislikes. We have so much in common as human beings, yet we have our unique cultures, beliefs, practices, and traditions. Before the internet, global travel, and immigration, we lived in more homogenous communities and were more likely to marry someone from our town or neighborhood, maybe even the boy or girl next door. My husband says his grandma used to say that each town furnishes its own mates. That's not the case today. Today the U.S. and Canada and other countries have become a mosaic of different cultures and religious groups. We work, live, and go to school with people from backgrounds very different from our own. The internet has facilitated our ability to meet people from all over the world, and from different backgrounds.. Online social groups enable us to develop relationships we would never have imagined before. All this sparks our interest in the possibility of marriage to people from backgrounds very different from our own. While we may be expanding our interest as we become more familiar with different groups, that may not be the case for our parents and extended family members. While diversity is amazing and exciting, cross-cultural communication and understanding may be challenging. Contact with each other in a common experience tends to increase ease of communication and understanding, however language barriers, growing up in different social contexts, and holding beliefs about racial and cultural superiority present barriers and make it difficult to foster appreciation and inclusion.

In addition to the ongoing racism and Islamophobia, during 2020 we witnessed the murder, among others, of George Floyd, a Black man in Minnesota, in broad daylight, captured on video and spread online around the world via social media. Because of the growth of the Black Lives Matter movement, global protests, the rise of hate crimes toward various groups, and the openness of the white supremacist movement, some have come to recognize the reality of race and racism in society and within the Muslim community, even while we continue to celebrate diversity.

The 1967 film *Guess Who's Coming to Dinner* brought to the big screen the issues of race and racism in marriage and how a perceived openly liberal family takes Joanna, their free-thinking white daughter's announcement of her engagement and introduction to her future husband, an African American doctor, John Prentice. Joanna's perspective of her parents was that they were very open and accepting of diversity. She was surprised to learn her parents were not as accepting of her engagement to a black man as she thought they would be. The movie shares the reactions of the young couple's family members to their relationship. Until the landmark 1967 civil-rights case Loving vs. Virginia, which was decided just five months before the movie was released, marriage between blacks and whites was illegal in many parts of the U.S.

That was 1967. This is 2021. Today in Muslim Student Association events and my *Before the Nikah* course sessions, I hear young Muslim men and women share their concern about their parent's view of their choice for who they want to marry. The young adults share their worry that their parents want them to marry someone from within their cultural community overseas rather than someone from the U.S. who is culturally or racially different from their families.

Race, racism, and our view of diversity before and during marriage play an important part in cultivating a healthy marriage and family. AmongMuslims are racially, culturally, linguistically, and religiously diverse families. One of my students shared having family members of different backgrounds and cultures around the world, a kind of United Nations family. My own family includes Muslims and Christians, African Americans, white Americans, European Germans, Arab Americans, West Indians, East Africans, and Latinos.

The important question is where do the two of you stand on most issues. Are you comfortable with the extended family you will most often interact with? Are you largely cohesive, mostly agreeable? Are you able to agree to disagree civilly and respectfully, or does diversity cause major disagreement and conflict? Are the differences in your extended family manageable so that you can maintain family ties and appreciate each other?

It will be important to assess your level of diversity congruence before the marriage. This is a real honest conversation before the nikah.

It may be important to have discussions around questions like which culture or racial background did your parents hope your spouse would be from? How does your family feel about other races and cultures compared to the culture of your family of origin? Did they have someone already selected for you? What kinds of phrases did you hear about other cultures or races when you were growing up? Would those phrases be considered ethnic slurs or racist today? Why is it so important to risk your relationship with your family to marry someone outside your culture or race if you know they are not supportive? Why is it so important to put your future spouse in a situation in which he or she may not be valued or accepted because their background is not loved by your family? Are you marrying someone outside your culture in hopes that you will be able to mold them into being like someone from your culture? What are your real expectations?

Consider the story of Harry and Meagan which provides a 2021 example of cross-cultural issues in marriage. Prince Harry and Meagan Markle married in 2018. Harry is a white European prince in the Royal Family in England with protocols on how people can meet his grandmother, the Queen. Meghan is an American actress. She is biracial, African American and White American. The couple faced and continue to face some real-life challenges regarding race and racial acceptance, which were revealed in an interview with Oprah Winfrey in the Spring of 2021 and reported in People Magazine and other news media. Behind the scenes, the couple said, although the royal family was initially "welcoming," tensions soon crept in, some with racist underpinnings. In one of the interview's most jaw-dropping moments, Meghan—the daughter of a white father and a Black Mother—revealed that there had been "concerns and conversations about how dark {Archie's skin} might be when he's born." Harry said these talks took place early in his romance with Meghan, well before they even had children. "There were obvious signs, even before we got married, that this was going to be really hard."

Consider these questions about Harry and Megan's story.

- What did Harry or Megan know before the marriage? What should they have discussed privately, with a professional pre-marital counselor to work out a plan of action, a strategy on how they would handle the racial challenges they would face?
- What didn't they know that would be important to know before marriage?
- What makes a healthy cross-cultural, interracial marriage?

Meghan and Harry's marriage is an example of the importance of addressing the red flashing, don't go warning flags and yellow pause flags related to race and culture before the marriage to reduce the problems that are likely to result during the marriage. Determine how you will both respond to racism and cross-cultural issues in your family and extended family prior to marriage in hopes of reducing the hurt and pain to having a harmonious peaceful marriage and family life. Or even though there is attraction and chemistry, perhaps the tools necessary for a healthy, long-lasting marriage are not available to your relationship and are not a good fit. It seems Megan and Harry love each other and are compassionate with each other. Their challenges may impact the peace and tranquility Allah reminds us is a core value for a healthy marriage.

TAKE ACTION

Engage in an honest personal cross-cultural assessment.

Which culture do you most identify with?

How do you describe yourself as regards your cultural, racial, faith, religious, and gender diversity dimensions?

Which culture or racial background did your parents hope your spouse would be from?

How does your family feel about other races and cultures compared to the culture of your family of origin?

Do they have someone already selected for you that they prefer you marry? Why is this their choice? Do you agree? If not, why not?

What kinds of phrases did you hear about other cultures or races when you were growing up? Would those phrases be considered ethnic slurs or racist today?

Why is it so important to risk your relationship with your family to marry someone outside your culture or race if you know they are not supportive?

Why is it so important to put your future spouse in a situation in which he or she may not be valued or accepted because their background is not loved by your family?

Are you marrying someone outside your culture in hopes that you will be able to mold them into being like someone from your culture? What are your real expectations?

In Summary

When the premarital process works, you are actually employing the Before the Nikah principles. The story below about Tahirah and Tarik demonstrates ways they incorporated the key Before the Nikah principles.

Four years ago, while in undergrad school, Tahirah took the *Before the Nikah* Marriage Preparation course. She recently graduated with her master's degree. She gave herself the summer after graduation to relax and chart her next course. Tahirah also decided to revisit and update her self-assessment, amend her ideal match profile, identified her Marriage Support Team, and decided she was ready to begin the path of choosing a life partner for marriage. The first night of Ramadan, Tahirah ran into her friends, Muhammad and Maria, at the masjid. They had known each other for years, having taken trips together, volunteered together, and been over at each other's homes. While they were catching up, Tahirah mentioned she was interested in getting married. Muhammad and Maria appreciated that Tahirah entrusted them with that information, offered to help, and prayed together with Tahirah that Allah would guide her through this journey. Muhammad and Maria were excited! They had been happily married for 8 years, felt the peace and happiness of their marriage, and prayed for the same for their friends. They also thought Tahirah was amazing and a great catch.

Also, in a city 40 minutes away was Tarik. The Spring before, he had just completed the *Before the Nikah* course. It turns out, he also was friends with Muhammad and Maria and they recommended he take the course. Muhammad and Maria had each engaged in a marriage preparation course and saw the benefits to their marriage. They had seen enough marriages go toxic and they were really motivated to give themselves a good start. Since Tariq and Muhammad worked together, they would drive together to Jummah prayer and grab lunch. But, since they were fasting after Jumu'ah, they had some extra time to just talk. Muhammad shared that he and Maria just attended a marriage rejuvenation retreat in Toronto to kick off Ramadan. Tarik was glad he brought up marriage because he had been wanting to ask Muhammad to be on his marriage success team. After taking the *Before the Nikah* course, Tarik continued to work on getting more organized with what it would take to get married and have a successful marriage. He outlined his list of values, he completed his self-assessment, and profile for his ideal compatible spouse. He assessed his finances. He had good income to take care of a family and had a good savings, so he was prepared to provide a mahr. So when Tarik asked Muhammad to be on his Marriage Success Team, he wholeheartedly agreed. He thought highly of Tarik and that he was a great catch.

That night Muhammad and Maria chatted at home, and he told her about Tarik's request. She and Muhammad simultaneously thought of Tahirah! Maria called up Tahirah and told her some details about Tarik and Muhammad called up Tarik to share information about Tahirah. So, when Muhammad and Maria held an iftar dinner party, they invited both Tarik and Tahirah. At the iftar all of the ladies gravitated toward each other and the guys toward each other to catch up on how Ramadan had been and the year, since they hadn't all been together since the previous Eid. At Magrib, Maria pulled Tahirah to pray next to her so she could point out who Tarik was so she could check him out through the night. Unbeknownst to Tahirah and Maria, Muhammed had already done the same to Tarik while they were getting the dates and fruit ready to break the fast. As the iftar wound down and the other guests left for taraweh prayer, Muhammad and Maria introduced Tarik to Tahirah. They chatted a bit and based on the information from Muhammad and Maria, they each thought it would be a good idea to continue to get to know each other.

Over the span of a year, they went through the vetting process checklist. They spent time getting to know each other's families and friends. They discussed the important questions they received from the tools in the *Before the Nikah* course to determine true compatibility related to their shared vision around spirituality, finances, personality, communication styles, intellectual mindset, and health matters. They went on a couple of road trips with Muhammad and Maria, including the beach and went to a conference hosted by a big national organization. At some point, Tarik invited Tahirah to attend a work picnic. Tahirah invited Tarik to a basketball game her work team was attending. They each enlisted their MST to do additional background checking. Both had grown up in the same state. But, Tarik went to college a few states away. Tahirah's MST helped her look into people who knew Tarik there. They spoke to an old roommate and his year's MSA president. Tarik's MST also inquired into Tahirah's background. She had been raised and studied in *the same state*. Tahirah and her mom gave Tarik a surprise visit at his home one Saturday. Tarik was pleasantly surprised.

It was not always a special occasion when they would meet up. It got to a point where Tarik would be over for dinner with Tahirah's family on a Tuesday. Tahirah's mom had even called up Tarik to help her with moving her office to her home after her movers bailed. He was gracious and prompt. Tarik's mom and Tahirah were in the same field. She asked Tahirah if she would be open to planning a dinner she was hosting for the president of an organization Tahirah had wanted to join. Tahirah was honored to get to be included in the prestigious event.

They gathered all of this information and then had regular check-in sessions with their MST about the information. And they gave the relationship time to see what patterns emerged in their interactions and if it would be healthy and compatible. Tarik and Tahirah each noticed the other being consistent with their word. They were in touch regularly, however, they were respectful of each other's boundaries and mindful of the other. Tahirah needed her sleep, as she was taking on a promotion at her job now that she graduated. So, when she told Tarik she needed to end the calls earlier now that she was moving into her new role, he understood and encouraged her. When Tahirah had a presentation to give at her job and was nervous and had to prepare for it, Tarik helped her prepare and then fully understood her need to have a few days alone to finish and complete it.

During their discussions about their health, Tarik shared that he had asthma and allergies. He has not lately, but in the past has had a serious asthma attack to the point where he had to crawl to a phone to get help. Usually, it is fine unless his allergies get stirred up with being around a cat, cat hair, or the weather really kicks up dust and pollen in the air. Tahirah loves cats. She did not have a cat at her parents' home but really wanted one. Tarik and Tahirah used the problem solving model that they learned in the course and came up with a solution they were comfortable with. So, they talked about whether or not they had a cat and how if they had a cat it would be one to not affect his allergies and asthma. This discussion went well.

Throughout the year, things went well. They used their resources. They made istikhara prayer. They had time to talk. Their talk was meaningful. They candidly addressed the hard questions. They did a background check. Their MST helped observe the interactions and assess the information they were receiving. They did not let them off the hook if they did not hear a clear answer to an important area. They helped Tarik and Tahirah stay awake. They helped them to not get lulled by the fact they were really starting to like each other. They helped them stay focused to get the answers they needed to know not just if they had chemistry, but that they would be compatible as life partners. Tarik and Tahirah gave the relationship time to develop, so they could observe patterns and if they were healthy or toxic. They got a gauge on each other's real intentions for getting married. They felt the sincerity and mutual kindness. They noticed they got along well. They could discuss challenging questions in a calm way. They felt comfortable and not anxious around each other. They did not have to tip toe or walk on eggshells about difficult topics. When they consulted their gut, it was at ease. They felt compassion and respect for each other. They got to KNOW each other and they liked each other.

When Ramadan came around again, Tarik and Tahirah were reflecting on where they were last Ramadan when they first met, and they were grateful to Allah. They made an appointment with a premarital counselor for some final help. They each called their attorney through their legal plan to discuss the legal implications of marriage in their life and discuss the process for getting a prenup. They scheduled an appointment with the Imam at Tahirah's mosque. And Tarik is ready to offer a mahr and buy a ring!

Throughout Tahirah and Tarik's story, we see their use of the key *Before the Nikah* principles. In summary, we have listed the 13 principles to refer to in the process of your matrimonial search. Remember to engage in these principles as you look for your lifelong partner.

1. Have a proactive prevention oriented mindset.
2. Participate in premarital education for singles.
3. Ensure informed consent.
4. Use The Vetting Process and conduct a background check.
5. Engage in a personal self-assessment to get to know yourself and be honest with yourself.
6. Learn and understand what the Qur'an and the married life of the Prophet show you about marriage.
7. Learn and use good communication skills.
8. Know your expectations and convey what you expect.

9. Take the time to truly get to know each other to determine if you are compatible.
10. Use your Marriage Support Team in the premarital phase to assist with the vetting process
11. Have zero tolerance for violence
12. Address money matters before the nikah
13. Address the legal aspects of marriage before the nikah

Part Two

Family and Community in the Healthy Marriage Movement

As a community, we must support marriage preparation efforts. Parents will want to consider prepaying for a marriage preparation course as a wedding gift for their children to assure a stronger foundation for their healthy marriage.

Dispense with the idea of rushing the marriage to avoid zina.

Let's teach the importance of taking time to prepare for a long lasting healthy marriage.

Let's not gaslight people who have a list of what they are looking for in their future spouse as being too picky. Try to see where they are coming from before you tell them what is important to them doesn't matter.

For example, a group of young women were talking. One of them said, "He doesn't speak Arabic like she does. The other young woman quickly dismissed her and said it didn't matter that he doesn't speak Arabic like she does. This young woman sees her culture as a very important part of herself and who she is. She loves the culture, the movies, and the music. That's her pastime. Having a spouse who also speaks

Arabic is important to her. Her parents are fluent in English, but they also speak Arabic.

Another example is of a young man who said he was looking for someone who is socially conscious. The other guys dismissed his interest, saying that didn't matter when looking to get married. But to this young man, it does matter, since he has plans to run for political office one day. He wants to marry someone who is social justice-minded.

A third example is that of a young woman who has one child and doesn't want to marry anyone who has children. Her friends said she should be open. But she knows she does not have the capacity to do justice to raising other children.

It is so important to listen to what people want and what they know about themselves.

Next Steps in The Healthy Muslim Marriage Movement

I believe in the important foundation a healthy marriage provides. Because I have stood firm on this belief for more than 20 years, despite the lack of community support and investment, I thought it was time to compile my perspectives and philosophies and provide an introduction to my course as recognition of the need for a proactive approach to healthy marriage.

The purpose of marriage in Islam is to help each other pass the tests in this life; to help each other get to Heaven. This life is for a brief time. It is filled with tests. And the Devil is constantly working to break up marriages and families. As Muslims, our goal is to work through the tests of this life, do good for God's sake, and earn His blessings, so we can get to enjoy the Paradise in the next life together.

So, it is so important to wisely choose a spouse that will help you get to live your best life and help you get to Heaven. I am a strong believer in personal spiritual development and personal emotional growth and development. I am also a believer in the benefits of premarital education, marriage preparation education, premarital counseling, as well as marriage education and counseling, and coaching and support throughout the marriage.

In this book, I have shared my thoughts and perspectives as a professional social worker with more than 40 years of experience working with children, youth, and families. My foundation is in the field of prevention, working to address issues before they become problems or intervene early on before they become irreparable. So, I do believe in phrases like, "An ounce of prevention is worth a pound of cure," and "a stitch in time really does save nine."

Before the Nikah is about why it's important to choose your spouse or lifelong partner wisely and why it is important to get educated and get prepared for marriage, so you know how to make a good selection. This book is about what marriage preparation is, what it does, and how it helps an individual seeking marriage make a wise choice in their future spouse and what it looks like when you're engaged in marriage preparation. This book is also about the real consequences of not engaging in marriage preparation. I have personally and professionally witnessed too many situations in which individuals married the wrong person. They married people who were not a good fit, not compatible, not right for them. They married without having knowledge about what it means to have and be in a healthy relationship or how to develop a healthy relationship and the kinds of skills that are needed to be loving, caring, compassionate, and have a peaceful union. Most people just don't know about this. They don't have any education that helps them know about what a healthy relationship really is, what it looks like, or how to make a good selection. I have talked about some of the consequences for the individual, the couple, the children, the community, the in-laws, and parents when you choose wrong. When we know the consequences of not preparing for marriage and not taking the premarital phase seriously, my hope is we will take marriage and preparation for it more seriously.

Increased knowledge and relationship skills will make an important difference in who we choose to marry and whether or not that relationship is loving and compassionate.

Another piece of the premarital phase discussed in this book is the vetting process and really taking time to understand and engage in weeding through information about the person that may be your prospective spouse. The thing is, when people present themselves, they often wear a mask. They are not the people that you will come to know. We put on our best face, our best outfit, and we wear some makeup. I mean this is what we as human beings do. When we are seeking a potential spouse, especially in these days and times, with society being such a global society and most of us not having grown up with the people we're considering for marriage, we have to engage in a rigorous vetting process. We must know the core criteria for marriage, what to look for, and how to vet those we meet and think we might like to marry. You do not know each other, so you have no real idea if you are going to be a good fit for each other. You do not know if you will have any of the characteristics on which to build the kind of marriage Allah speaks about in the Qur'an regarding being loving, compassionate, and peaceful. Since you do not know each other, you will want to spend time learning about each other. You will want to learn how best to determine the kind of person you are talking with, to determine if they are honest and whether you will be a good fit for one another.

Blind trust is really a big problem, especially when there are narcissistic abusers, hypocrites, and green card scammers in the pool with empathetic, thoughtful, honest, and sincere people. They all look the same at first. Initially, we do not see any difference. Many of us are sincere but because not everyone is, it is very important to remember to take time to get to know the person you are exploring for marriage.

It is essential to discuss marital readiness and determine if you are ready for marriage? Is the other person ready for marriage? Are you compatible and ready to marry each other?

*Before the Nikah for Parents, Imams
and Community Leaders*

I have been writing and speaking about the importance of premarital education and marriage preparation, as well as teaching young Muslim men and women who have been students of my *Before the Nikah Marriage Preparation Course* for approximately 20 years.

When I started writing, I decided that this book is not only about what singles should know before marriage, but it is also about what parents, imams and community leaders need to do to help our children, single people, and community members have a good start for a healthy marriage. They need to have parent and community support. I can teach philosophies, principles, and skills needed to prepare for a healthy marriage, but it is important for their parents and community to be aware of the reality of the matrimonial scene and what it is like for our single community members who want to get married and have a healthy long-lasting marriage today.

We need to have our eyes open to what is leading to the increasing divorce rate and more than that, the dysfunctional and toxic relationships so many are experiencing within marriage. We also need to be aware of how difficult it is for our single community members to find good spouses who are compatible with them. The search for a good person to marry and have a loving, fulfilling relationship with is difficult today. Many have reached their late thirties and given up. Our sisters are increasingly disappointed about the prospects of meeting someone who will be compatible, kind, loving, and a good provider.

The single members of our community need our help. They need the help of their parents, community leaders, and imams. The future of our families and communities is at stake. They need us to be trusted advisors, guiding them in one of the most significant areas of their life.

Fifty percent of couples in the larger society are divorced. The divorce rate for Muslims is thirty-three percent. Thankfully, there are happy couples who love each other and have a peaceful relationship, but sadly there are also those who remain in unhappy, unfilled, and toxic relationships.

A toxic, dysfunctional relationship can wreak havoc on the couple, the children if there are any, the couple's parents, their siblings, their friends, and their community. Friends will often have to choose sides and decide which one to invite to the dinner party and who they need to leave off the invitation list. Grandparents are not able to see their grandchildren. Children are split between their parents. In a bad break up and custody battle, children sometimes blame themselves for their parent's problems. They are often traumatized by the mean-spirited relationship they witness between their parents. A loving joint custody relationship is ideal, but often children are used as pawns in a custody battle.

My Own Experience

My parents divorced when I was about ten years old. Before they divorced, I witnessed them being emotionally and physically abusive toward each other. They separated. They reconciled. They separated. Eventually, they divorced. My mother, brothers, and I moved back and forth from Queens to Brooklyn. And we went to a few different elementary schools during this time. I was glad when we were able to settle down in Brooklyn long enough so that I was able to stay in one high school. Even though I didn't much like the area we lived in, I was able to make good high school friends that I am still in touch with almost fifty years later. While I was about 8 years old, I remember sitting on the steps of my grandmother's home where we lived in Queens, crying and thinking I was the only kid going through this drama, witnessing her parents break up and hurt each other. Choosing a social work career, I learned that I was one of many children experiencing this.

Of course, I thought I would never repeat this pattern and put my children through some of the experiences I faced growing up. The thing is, when you don't know better, you repeat the same behaviors you grew up seeing. I was reluctant to get married because of the experiences I saw as a child. Alhamdulillah, eventfully I was blessed to marry a good person. We still had our challenges and some bumps along the way. We had to grow up and learn some life lessons, like the importance of our faith as our foundation, the importance of good communication, and the importance of working continuously to build our relationship.

So, after breaking up and learning some lessons, we reconciled and remarried. With God's blessings, education, spiritual and emotional maturity, we grew up. Had we been educated about what it takes to make a healthy marriage before our first marriage, perhaps we could have avoided some of the pitfalls that led to our divorce.

Lessons I Want to Pass On

I learned a few lessons from my personal life experiences and professionally working in the field. I also learned that single people today have as many, if not more challenges than we did. Some of the lessons I learned convinced me that:

1. To have a successful marriage, it is key that we practice what Prophet Muhammad taught us. That is, "Tie our camel and rely on Allah." It is essential that we proactively do our part to prepare for marriage as we rely on Allah.

2. The goal of a successful Muslim marriage is to help each other get to Heaven. To have a successful marriage, a solid, spiritual foundation is essential; relying on Allah's guidance.

3. Even though single people think their relationship is just about the two of them, it is not. They bring the unresolved challenges of their childhood and/or their previous relationships into their marriage as well.

4. Generally single folks across today's generations do not have the knowledge, relationship skills, and emotional maturity needed for a healthy married life. These are things that can be developed and learned, but it takes focused effort to do so.

5. Everyone is not well suited for each other. A serious, well thought out assessment of the couple exploring marriage by a professional in marriage education or counseling is needed before we so quickly pair people up. Chemistry is only one part of it. It is an important part, but temperament, philosophy, religious perspective, hopes and dreams for the future, messages received, and things observed as children, also play an important part in how compatible we are for each other. True compatibility according to Aya Rasheed includes the physical aspects of attraction and health, intellectual connection around education and political views, the emotional aspect of respect and communication style, as well as a shared vision around spirituality and religion, financial view, life priorities, cleanliness and orderliness, and sociability.

6. We also live in a global society. We are meeting so many people in online communities and different platforms who are strangers. And even if we spend time in online networking, we really don't get to know the person behind Facebook or Instagram until we take the relationship offline and spend time talking with them, observing them, and truly listening to them.

7. Our community is diverse racially, ethnically, linguistically, in the ways we practice our religion and our experiences growing up. Most of us didn't grow up on the same block, neighborhood, village, or city. Our views and perspectives are often quite different. Even though we may identify with the same religion we may not understand or practice our faith in the same way. All of this is impacting single people as they explore prospects for marriage.

8. We also live in an age of entitlement and narcissism. Empathy and compassion are hard to come by. It is so important to gain knowledge of these behaviors, beware, and really take

time to vet for these characteristics, so that you avoid the narcissistic behaviors.

9. People lie. I take no pleasure in this reality. I didn't want to believe it or acknowledge it. But even outwardly, religious people who don traditional religious attire, the beard, and may give considerable donations are not always sincere. They lie about who they are and who their children are. Honesty seems to be harder to come by these days but necessary when deciding who you want to marry.

10. Most people enter marriage with little if any education about the dynamics of relationships and how to cultivate a healthy, loving relationship in marriage. Nor do they realize that these are skills that can be learned in a course of study. People often say there are no books about marriage. But there are actually books about healthy marriage and relationship skills that can be studied and put into practice.

11. The support, mentorship, and guidance needed is not available to those getting married. It takes the support of knowledgeable, trusted advisors. It takes a supportive village for a couple to be successful. Our community does have people who care, but they are not knowledgeable about how to navigate courtship, screen for toxicity, and negotiate the mahr. Also, so many are guided by culture rather than a broad and balanced religious understanding. It is important to realize that many of our mentors teach by culture or mix culture and religion. Not enough consideration is given to the social context in which we live. So, it is difficult to distinguish between Herslam, Hislam, and Islam.

12. People are marrying people they don't know. They really don't KNOW much about each other. Often their conversations are shallow and not about the real things that will matter in marriage. More is based on what looks good on

paper and physical appearance rather than the content of their character and heart.

13. It takes TIME to get to KNOW each other and whether you are compatible. Time needs to be spent getting answers to the important questions about your expectations and vision for your future life together. It needs to be spent vetting to determine the person is who he or she says she is, assessing compatibility, and readiness for marriage. I grew up hearing the phrase "more haste, less speed." I learned that rushing causes missteps and causes us to miss important details or engage in confirmation bias. Encourage our singles to take time getting to know each other.

14. Muslims tend to have children soon after marriage, if He wills that blessing for you. Consider waiting two years after marriage before getting pregnant. Use these first two years to build your relationship as a couple and with Allah before you bring children into the world. Take a parenting skills training course. Bring children into a settled, stable home where as a couple you have started your marriage off on a good foot and a good foundation, a home filled with sakinah, compassion, and love. Parents may want you to have children so they can become grandparents but know that more than anything they want you and your children to be healthy and safe. Give yourself time to settle in the role of spouse before you take on the role of parent. There are a lot of changes, hormonal, and emotional that you both go through during pregnancy. The stressors of married life, moving to a new area, securing employment, and pregnancy put a lot on a new couple. Give it consideration.

15. As parents, imams, and community leaders we have a long overdue responsibility to guide, protect, and help our children, our single brothers and sisters, choose wisely and vet their prospective spouses for compatibility. It is important to

help them pay attention to their intuition, identify the red flags and warning signs Allah provides to make good choices as they seek a healthy marriage. Knowing that we want solid, healthy communities that are strong and intact, we must commit to the Healthy Marriage Movement.

What needs to be done?
What can be done?

It is our responsibility to provide support and education for our single people about this significant aspect of their lives.

Parents who are willing to pay thousands of dollars on planning a wedding for their children want to ensure their investment by designating a percentage of the wedding budget for marriage preparation, premarital education, and premarital counseling which Inshaallah will provide a positive return on their investment. It is time to support, encourage, and expect our children to get educated about what Islam has taught us about what makes a healthy marriage.

Those exploring marriage need education, support, and help choosing wisely and seriously vetting prospects. One of the things our community must recognize is that our single community members and our children are not marrying the boy or girl next door. They're not marrying someone they grew up with. They are likely going to marry someone you don't know and they don't know. A thorough vetting process is essential whether they marry someone from your hometown or not. Recognizing that there are so many different types of people in society today is essential. Sadly, too many people don't tell the truth. It is important not to fill in the blanks or create a narrative to make your prospective spouse what you want him or her to be. Don't assume that what the prospect is saying is true without verifying what they have told you. I know it is difficult because most of us have been taught to give 70 excuses and to cover our brother's and sister's faults. We have also been taught we have a responsibility to be honest when we are asked about someone for the purpose of business or marriage. Also the Qur'an is clear that there are believers, disbelievers, and hypocrites. The latter of which say they believe when they don't. So, it is essential to determine where the prospective falls before you trust him or her with your family. Remember when you agree to marriage you not only bring your spouse into your life but your family's life.

The Healthy Marriage Movement

I believe we all need to join the Healthy Marriage Movement in the larger society and promote it within our own Muslim communities. Because marriage is the primary unit and cornerstone of society, we need to focus on it. The time is now to end drive-by nikahs and spontaneous marriage ceremonies in the imam's office just after Friday prayers. The time is now to put an end to quickie marriage ceremonies with a wali and witnesses who don't know the bride or groom. The time is now to end the excuse that mandating marriage preparation will cause community members to engage in premarital sex because they don't have the self control or value marriage enough to wait, learn, and commit to a lifelong healthy marriage.

It is time we all lock arms and commit to preparation and education before marriage. As parents, those helping people get married, it is important to raise our children knowing that marriage is so important that they must learn relationship skills, understand the purpose of marriage as Muslims, and know how to select someone who will be a good fit for their dunya and their akhirah. They need to know how to put Allah at the foundation of marriage, and how to vet for good character and compatibility.

It is important that we recognize our children and single community members, some of whom may be new converts, are in a different place and time, and under different societal circumstances than we had. It is important that we as parents, aunties and uncles, older brothers and sisters, grow and understand what our role is as wali. This is a huge responsibility that does not end with the selection of a prospective spouse or the conclusion of the marriage ceremony. Cultivating healthy marriage takes time and mentorship, wise elders and family support, not interference or meddling. People need a MST or Marriage Support Team whose members are knowledgeable, wise, caring, and supportive advisors.

As members of the MST, our job is to become educated about marriage in these days and times, the challenges, tools for success, and to learn about the example set by the Prophet Muhammad, peace be upon him. Our job is to learn what it means to support our friends and family in their marriage process based on our faith. Marriage is not a haphazard endeavor. It is not a hook 'em up where you just throw two people together. It should be compatible and successful for them.

Over the years, I have learned that many imams are reluctant to mandate premarital preparation, education, and counseling before marriage out of concern that it will serve as an obstacle to marriage and promote premarital sex because the couple would be unable to control themselves over the duration of preparation process. So instead, the philosophy of many of our imams and families is to rush the couple to marry rather than to have them step back and learn what they are getting into and how to make it successful. And it is a disaster. Consequently, and sadly, after a few months or a few short years, the same imam who officiated the nikah ceremony, now has to sign the divorce papers. Folks are all in for the wedding but not available when issues arise and so couples are left high and dry when the marriage turns sour. In most cases, education, time, and a serious vetting process can make the difference and prevent many of the issues couples face and the abrupt end to the marriage.

Throughout North America let us raise our voices in our homes, in our mosques, and in our communities to promote zero tolerance for domestic violence, and to promote premarital preparation, marriage enrichment, and counseling resources. As well, let us work together to build coalitions and strategic partnerships between mosques, imams, mental health professionals, community leaders, and parents to develop a strong effort toward good selection of spouses and a commitment to healthy marriage.

Do not:

- Make the wife the debtor for her mahr.
- Rush marriage to prevent zina.
- Pass off abuse as cultural.
- Gamble with marriage.
- Enable abuse or abusers.
- Be naïve. Get educated.
- Introduce people for marriage who are not suited for each other.
- Continue to try to fit round pegs into square holes.
- Stigmatize divorced people or single parents as poor candidates for marriage.
- Discourage people from discerning about their choices for a future spouse.

Do:

- Support the Healthy Muslim Marriage Movement.
- Plan healthy halal ways for single Muslims to meet.
- Get educated. Singles get premarital education.
- Get educated. Parents, learn how to best support your young adult children in choosing wisely.
- Get educated. Learn how to support our brothers and sisters who are recent converts to Islam and want to get married when the time is right and they meet someone who is compatible.

- Parents do encourage your children to learn about marriage in Islam, relationship building skills andcommunication skills as early as high school.
- Parents do begin a mahr fund for your sons.
- Candidly, discreetly, and honestly tell the truth when sincerely asked regarding those planning to marry.
- Engage in family planning. Do consider delaying pregnancy for at least the first two years of your marriage to build a solid relationship as a couple and engage in parenting skills training.
- Engage in due diligence when vetting your prospective spouse. Conduct a thorough assessment and evaluation.

TAKE ACTION

Organizations, community leaders, mosque leaders, imams: take action to promote healthy marriage.

- Commit to the Healthy Muslim MarriageMovement.
- Sign on to the Healthy Marriage Community Covenant initiated by Muslim Alliance in North America and the Islamic Social Services Association in 2010.
- Participate in the National Healthy Muslim Marriage Week during the first week of Ramadan each year hosted by the Islamic Social Services Association-USA.
- Require a minimum of 3 hours of premarital education before the imam of the mosque agrees to officiate the nikah ceremony.
- Encourage 6 hours of premarital education prior to the nikah ceremony.
- Require a written and signed Islamic marriage contract.
- Recognize that a state marriage license is necessary to activate state and federal benefits of marriage.
- Provide opportunities for couple support and enrichment.
- Support zero tolerance for domestic abuse.
- Demonstrate, support, and value Muslim professionals in social work, marriage and family therapy, and counseling.
- Collaborate with professional social workers, counselors, and marriage and family therapists to provide accessible premarital preparation and education services, as well as ongoing marriage counseling and enrichment services in the local community.

Parents

- Educate yourself about ways to assist your children in preparing for marriage.
- Start a mahr account when your son is born and encourage him to fund it with his allowance and income as he gets older. The more he invests in his mahr account inshaallah, the more seriously he will take marriage and his responsibility to his future wife and family.
- Make premarital education, counseling, and marriage preparation an expectation in your family and part of your family culture.
- Demonstrate the value of professional as well as spiritually based premarital and marriage counseling.
- Role model healthy relationships and healthy communication skills.
- Continue to model marriage enrichment by attending couples' retreats, date nights, vacations, and counseling.
- When marriage is not healthy after all efforts to work on it, dissolve amicably with ihsan.

Summary

Helping those who want to get married choose wisely is an amana or trust. This is a responsibility we all have. As a single person, make it your responsibility to get marriage education. As a parent, encourage your children to engage in a course of study about marriage before they have selected someone they want to marry. As imams, you are front line to helping to educate and assess marital readiness. Partner with the professionals in your community to help our single community members become better prepared for marriage. Commit to requiring premarital education before officiating marriages. Use the time at the minbar to strengthen our community with messages about the married life of Prophet Muhammad (pbuh) to commit to Healthy Marriages with love, compassion, and sakinah.

References

Abugideiri, S. and Magid, M. (2013). Before You Tie the Knot. Amazon.com

Ali, B. (2011). Why "Half Our Deen.com". Muslimmatters.org.

Al-Heeti, A. (2019). Beyond Tinder: How Muslim millennials are looking for love. CNET.com

Alwani, Z. and Abugideri, S. (2003) What Islam says about Domestic Violence: A Guide for Helping Muslim Families. Virginia: Foundation for Appropriate and Immediate Temporary Help (FAITH).

Domestic Abuse Statistics. Peaceful Families Project. peacefulfamilies.org/statistics.html.

Durvasula, R. (2019). Don't You Know Who I Am? New York: A Post Hill Press Book.

Ezzeldine, M. (2019). Before the Wedding. California: Izza Publishing.

Glatsky, G. (2017). Mosques takes on matchmaking of Black Muslim women. The Philadelphia Inquirer.

Hauslohner, A. (2018). Muslim, millennial and single: A generation struggles to find love. Washington Post.

Khattab, M. The Clear Quran. Illinois: Book of Signs Foundation.

Killawi, A.,et al. (2017). Perceptions and experiences of marriage preparation among U.S. Muslim: Multiple voices from the community. Journal of Marital and Family Therapy. American Association for Marriage and Family Therapy.

Killawi, A., et al. (2014). Promoting Healthy Marriages & Preventing Divorce in the American Muslim Community. Institute for Social Policy and Understanding. www.ispu.org/social-policy/marriage-and-divorce/

Maqsood, R. (1998). The Muslim Marriage Guide. New Delhi: Goodword.

Nadir, A (1998). Promoting Positive Marital Outcomes Among Muslims in America. In Islam in America: Images and Challenges. Indianapolis: University of Indianapolis Press.

Nadir, Z. and Nadir, A. (2012). Laying down the law: What women should know about the legal side of marriage. Azizah Magazine (Vol 7, Issue 2). Atlanta: WOW Publishing, Inc.

Naeem, Z. (2008). Jihad of the Soul. Michigan: The Niyah Company.

Preventing Intimate Partner Violence. (2020) National Center for Injury Prevention and Control, Division of Violence Prevention. https://www.cdc.gov/violenceprevention/intimatepartnerviolence/fastfact.html

Smith, L. (2020). Dare to Get Rich: Shorten Your Learning Curve. Book Ripple Publishing Press.

Tauber, M. (2021). Meghan & Harry's Bombshell Interview: Our Side of the Story. People Magazine. March 22, 2021.

Glossary

Alhamdulilah: English transliteration for the Arabic; meaning: All praise be to God.

Akhirah: The Hereafter

Allah: Arabic word for God, literally the One God.

Al-Baqara: The Cow, Chapter 2 of the Qur'an

Al-Ma'un: The Small Kindnesses

Ar-Rum- The Romans- Chapter 20 of the Qur'an

Du'a: Prayer, supplication

Dunya: Worldly life. The current life on earth

Hadith: Sayings of the Prophet Muhammad (pbuh) and narrations about his behavior

Ihsan: Behaving with excellence, in the context of marriage it refers to treating your spouse with the utmost care and kindness

InshaAllah/inshaallah: God willing, If God wills

Imam: Muslim clergy, also refers to a person

Jennah, Jannah: Paradise, Heaven

Mahr: obligation given from groom to bride as a legal condition of Islamic marriage. May be in the form of money, jewelry, real estate, furniture, gold or other valuables, wealth

Masjid: mosque, Muslim place of worship

Muwaddah: Love and compassion

Nikah: Islamic Marriage Contract

Qur'an: Holy book for Muslims, considered to be the Word of God, translated into many languages

Rahma: Compassion

Salaam: Peace

Sunnah: The way of the Prophet Muhammad (pbuh) captured in his sayings & recorded deeds

Seerah: History of the Prophet Muhammad (pbuh)

Surah: Chapter

Taqwa: Being ever-conscious of Allah

Wali: Guardian

Acknowledgements

I thank Allah, the Creator, for enabling me to write this book after teaching these principles to singles and newlyweds over the past two decades.

I am grateful that this time around I was guided to make a wise choice and was blessed with Karim Nadir, his support, encouragement and reminders that my work in the field of marriage education is meaningful and should be pursued.

I have appreciated the lessons I have learned and the invaluable discussions I have had with my sons Yerodin Nadir, Dahir Nasser and my daughter in law, Aya Rasheed about life and healthy relationships that contributed to the lessons and stories I share in this book.

I am fortunate to have had the opportunity to work with my daughter Zarinah Nadir in many capacities as community workers, trainers and so much more. She continues to help me grow the Before the Nikah Institute and Marriage Preparation Course and complete this book. Thank you Zarinah for creatively and critically thinking about the challenges singles face and the best ways to convey the material.

Thank you to my parents and my siblings. You taught me the value of family through the ups and downs which inspire my commitment to the Healthy Marriage Movement.

Thank you to my dear sister friends Frieda Muwakkil, Karen Hadley, Marci Hadley-Mariel, and Della Aman. Thank you for the years of encouragement and prayers, for believing in this work and for cheering me on to the finish line.

Many thanks to the graduates, alumni and future students of the Before the Nikah Marriage Preparation Course. You have inspired the publication of this book for others beyond the course to experience what you found so valuable.

I am forever grateful to the guest faculty and graduation speakers who have helped convey the course objectives that are now chapters and principles provided in this book- Zarinah Nadir, Archie Aquino, Susan Werhle, Latisha Ojuriye, Lisa Hashem, Angelica Lindsey-Ali, Aya Rasheed, Salma Abugideri, Baba Ali, Imam Nadim Ali, and Imam Mohamed Magid.

Thank you to alumni and teaching assistants- Estu Arifianti, Shaunice Lacey, Samantha Hill, Sabreen Azhar and Omaima Faris. Your contributions to the course have made all the difference.

Everyone needs coaches and mentors to guide them and encourage them. I have had the best- Shahina Siddiqui, Carol Coles Henry, Clay Dix, Stephanie Nowak, Dr Kahkshan Ali, Craig Hephner, Tanisha Morgan, Harold Branch and Tony Agurs. You inspired me to press on in the different areas of my life which has culminated in the publication of this book and the me I am today.

Thank you to Leanna Abdelmaged for being a beta reader, starting the editing process and motivating not to give up.

Special thanks to the Book Power Academy team, my editors, my fellow Power Authors and my writing coach and publisher Zarinah El-Amin. I am grateful for the guidance and inspiration you provided that led me to dust my twenty year old manuscript off, revive it and bring it publication for singles everywhere.

In loving memory of Dr. Cheryl El-Amin, a fellow social worker and my friend. I am grateful for the conversations, the opportunities to coauthor articles and book chapters and work for healthy families and communities.

Salaam/ Peace,
Dr. Aneesah Nadir

Appendix 

100 questions by Imam Magid
Pre-Marital Questionnaire
Source: Abugideiri and Magid (2013)

1.   What is your concept of marriage?
2.   Have you ever been married before?
3.   Are you married now?
4.   What are your expectations of marriage?
5.   What are your goals in life? Long-term and short-term plans.
6.   Identify three things that you want to accomplish in the near future.
7.   Identify three things that you want to accomplish long-term.
8.   Why have you chosen me as your potential spouse?
9.   What is the role of religion in your life – now?
10.   10. Are you a spiritual person?
11.   What is your understanding of an Islamic marriage?
12.   What are you expecting of your spouse, religiously?
13.   What is your relationship between yourself and the Muslim community in your area?

14. Are you volunteering in any Islamic activities?
15. What can you offer your mate, spiritually?
16. What is the role of a husband?
17. What is the role of a wife?
18. Do you want to practice polygny?
19. What is your relationship with your family?
20. What do you expect your relationship to be like with the family of your spouse?
21. What do you expect the relationship between your spouse and your family to be like?
22. Is there anyone in your family that lives with you now?
23. Are you planning to have anyone in your family live with you in the future?
24. If for any reason my relationship with your family turns sour, what should be done?
25. Who are your friends? Identify at least three.
26. How did you get to know them?
27. Why are they your friends?
28. What do you like most about them?
29. What will your relationship with them be like after marriage?
30. Do you have friends from the opposite sex?
31. What is the level of your relationship with them – now?
32. What will be the level of your relationship with them after marriage?
33. What type of relationship do you want your spouse to have with your friends?
34. What are the things that you do in your free time?
35. Do you like to have guests in your home for entertainment?
36. What are you expecting from your spouse when your friends come to the house?
37. What is your opinion of speaking other languages in the home that I do not understand? With friends? With family?
38. Do you travel?

39. How do you spend your vacations?

40. How do you think your spouse should spend vacations?

41. Do you read?

42. What do you read?

43. After marriage, do you think that you are one to express romantic feelings verbally?

44. After marriage, do you think that you want to express affection in public?

45. How do you express your admiration for someone that you know – now?

46. How do you express your feelings to someone who has done a favor for you?

47. Do you like to write your feelings?

48. If you wrong someone, how do you apologize?

49. If someone has wronged you, how do you want them to apologize to you?

50. How much time passes before you choose to forgive someone?

51. How do you make important and less important decisions in your life?

52. Do you use foul language at home? In public? With your family?

53. Do your friends use foul language?

54. Does your family use foul language?

55. How do you express anger?

56. How do you expect your spouse to express anger?

57. What do you do when you are angry?

58. When do you think it is appropriate to initiate mediation in a marriage?

59. When there is a dispute in your marriage, religious or not, how should the conflict be resolved?

60. Define mental, verbal, emotional, and physical abuse.

61. What would you do if you felt that you had been abused?

62. Who would you call for assistance if you were being abused?

63. Do you suffer from any chronic disease or condition?
64. Are you willing to take a physical exam by a physician before marriage?
65. What is your understanding of proper health and nutrition?
66. How do you support your own health and nutrition?
67. What is your definition of wealth?
68. How do you spend your money?
69. How do you save your money?
70. How do you think that your use of money will change after marriage?
71. Do you have any debts now? If so, how are you making progress to eliminate the debt?
72. Do you use credit cards?
73. Do you support the idea of taking loans to buy a home?
74. What are you expecting from your spouse financially?
75. What is your financial responsibility in a marriage?
76. Do you support the idea of a working wife?
77. If so, how do you think a dual-income family should manage funds?
78. Do you currently use a budget to manage your finances?
79. Who are the people to whom you are financially responsible?
80. Do you support the idea of utilizing baby-sitters and maids?
81. Do you want to have children? If not, why?
82. To the best of your understanding, are you able to have children?
83. Do you want to have children in the first two years of marriage? If not, then when?
84. Do you believe in abortion in you family?
85. Do you have children now?
86. What is your relationship with your children now?
87. What is your relationship with their parents now?
88. What relationship do you expect your spouse to have with your children and their parents?

89. What is the best method of raising children?

90. What is the best method of disciplining children?

91. How were you raised?

92. How were you disciplined?

93. Do you believe in spanking children? Under what circumstances?

94. Do you believe in public schools for your children?

95. Do you believe in Islamic schools for your children?

96. Do you believe in homeschooling your children? If so, by whom?

97. What type of relationship should your children have with non-Muslim classmates and friends?

98. Would you send your children to visit their extended family if they lived in another state or country?

99. What type of relationship do you want your children to have with all of their grandparents?

100. If there are members of your family that are not Muslim, that are of a different culture or race, what type of relationship do you want to have with them?

Steps I can take to handle my
Angry Feelings during a Conflict

I can....

- Take 3 Deep Cleansing Breaths
- Agree on a Time Out
- If I'm standing, sit down
- If I'm sitting lay down
- Make cold wudu/ablution
- Pray
- Meditate
- Remember the tradition of Shura/ Mutual Consultation
- Review the good lessons we have been taught in Qur'an and the examples set by the Prophet (pbuh)
    - He (pbuh), would listen attentively to those who spoke in his presence.
    - He (pbuh), would turn his whole self toward the person he was listening to.
    - He (pbuh) demonstrated respect for young, old, men and women, and people with disabilities.
- Review and adhere to good agreements we have set.

The Problem Solving Process

- Start with Bismillah/ In the Name of God
- Recite Surah Al Fatiha together
- Identify the Problem
- Brainstorm ways to address the difficulty
- Choose a solution
- Monitor
- Revise if needed
- End with dua/ Sura Asr

Istikhara Prayer for Seeking Guidance

Translation

"O Allah, verily I seek the better [of either choice] from You, by Your knowledge, and I seek ability from You, by Your power, and I ask You from Your immense bounty. For indeed You have power, and I am powerless; You have knowledge and I know not; You are the Knower of the unseen realms. O Allah, if You know that this matter is good for me with regard to my religion, my livelihood and the end of my affair then decree it for me, facilitate it for me, and grant me blessing in it. And if You know that this matter is not good for me with regard to my religion, my livelihood and the end of my affair then turn it away from me and me from it; and decree for me better than it, wherever it may be, and make me content with it."

About Author

D r Aneesah Nadir, CEO and President of Dr Aneesah Nadir and Associates, LLC is an educator and family life coach. As a social worker with over 42 years experience and a prevention specialist she is passionate about teaching her Before the Nikah Marriage Preparation Course students how to prevent marriage problems and live a loving, compassionate, peaceful life. Dr Aneesah has a Doctor of Philosophy of Social Work Degree from Arizona State University where she taught for 17 years. Thousands of junior college and university level students of diverse backgrounds have studied the profession of social work under her and have been mentored by her. Dr Aneesah combines her love of teaching, social work, and her concern for the state of our families and communities. Her *Before the Nikah Marriage Preparation Course* enables her to teach about a subject she loves while making a difference in the lives of families and communities.

As a cofounder and the President of the Islamic Social Services Association, Inc. Dr Aneesah oversaw the start of the Sakinah Healthy Marriage Initiative, National Muslim Marriage Week and the Healthy Muslim Marriage Movement which is a growing movement in the U.S.A and Canada. She has served as the President of ISSA-U.S for 21 years. For her years of community service and pioneering work in the field of social work and Muslim Mental Health Dr. Aneesah was awarded the 2018 Black Muslim Psychology Conference Pioneer Award, the 2017 Islamic Society of North America Community Service Award, the 2019 Council on American Islamic Relations-AZ Community Service Award and the Center for Muslim Mental Health and Islamic Psychology 2019 Muslim Mental Health Professional Award. She is a speaker, teacher, and author.

In May 2021 Dr Nadir was recognized as the 2021 Businesswoman of the Year by the Tempe Chamber of Commerce in Arizona, for her work in the field of business and entrepreneurship!

On a personal note, Dr. Nadir was blessed to remarry her husband Karim after a short three years apart to mature and learn some important life lessons. The second time around the couple has been married for 30 years plus the original 10 for a total of 40 years and have grown in their love, faith, and family. Together they have four adult children, an amazing daughter in law and three grandchildren. Dr. Aneesah loves spending time with her family and enjoying time with and mentoring young people as well as up and coming professionals.

For more information about the *Before the Nikah* course schedule, the Healthy Marriage Community Covenant, private appointments, coaching sessions, and to schedule speaking engagements email Dr Aneesah Nadir at **draneesah@gmail.com**